Perpetuating Inequality: Exploring the Role of the Indian Caste System

Copyright Page

TITLE: Perpetuating Inequality: Exploring the Role of the Indian Caste System

1ST Edition

Copyright @ 2023

Roberto M. Rodriguez. All rights reserved.

ISBN: 9798223466390

Table of Contents

Perpetuating Inequality: Exploring the Role of the Indian Caste System.. 1

Chapter 1: The Impact of the Indian Caste System on Access to Education.. 4

Chapter 2: The Role of the Indian Caste System in Perpetuating Social Inequality.. 14

Chapter 3: Intersectionality and the Indian Caste System: Examining the Experiences of Women and Marginalized Communities.............. 26

Chapter 4: The Historical Origins and Evolution of the Indian Caste System... 36

Chapter 5: The Economic Consequences of the Indian Caste System on Different Social Classes 46

Chapter 6: Religious Justifications and Interpretations of the Indian Caste System 56

Chapter 7: Caste-based Politics: Analyzing the Influence of Caste in Indian Elections and Governance 65

Chapter 8: Dalit Empowerment Movements and Resistance Against the Indian Caste System 75

Chapter 9: The Impact of Globalization on the Indian Caste System.. 84

Chapter 10: International Perspectives on the Indian Caste System: Comparisons with Other Forms of Discrimination............................ 96

Perpetuating Inequality: Exploring the Role of the Indian Caste System

By Roberto Miguel Rodriguez

Title: Perpetuating Inequality: Exploring the Role of the Indian Caste System

Introduction:

Welcome to the subchapter titled "Perpetuating Inequality: Exploring the Role of the Indian Caste System." In this section, we will delve into the intricate dynamics of the Indian caste system and its profound impact on various aspects of society. As sociologists, it is crucial for us to understand the origins, consequences, and contemporary manifestations of this deeply rooted social structure. By examining the role of the Indian caste system, we aim to shed light on the complex issues surrounding access to education, social inequality, intersectionality, historical evolution, economic consequences, religious justifications, political influence, resistance movements, globalization, and international perspectives.

The Impact of the Indian Caste System on Access to Education:

One of the most significant consequences of the Indian caste system is its effect on access to education. We will explore how caste-based discrimination hinders marginalized communities, particularly Dalits, from accessing quality education. By examining the disparities in educational opportunities, we can better understand the perpetuation of social inequality and the challenges faced by historically marginalized groups.

The Role of the Indian Caste System in Perpetuating Social Inequality:

This section will focus on how the Indian caste system perpetuates social inequality by creating a hierarchical society. We will analyze the caste-based division of labor, restrictions on inter-caste marriage, and the unequal distribution of resources. By examining these factors, we can uncover the mechanisms that sustain social stratification and hinder social mobility.

Intersectionality and the Indian Caste System: Examining the Experiences of Women and Marginalized Communities:

Through an intersectional lens, we will explore how the Indian caste system disproportionately affects women and other marginalized communities. By analyzing the intersecting oppressions of gender, caste, and class, we can gain insights into the unique challenges faced by these individuals and the need for inclusive social reforms.

The Historical Origins and Evolution of the Indian Caste System:

To understand the present, we must study the past. This section will delve into the historical origins and evolution of the Indian caste system. By tracing its roots, we can gain a comprehensive understanding of how it has evolved over time and adapted to changing social, political, and economic contexts.

The Economic Consequences of the Indian Caste System on Different Social Classes:

This section will explore the economic consequences of the Indian caste system on different social classes. We will analyze how caste-based discrimination affects economic opportunities, wealth distribution, and social mobility. By examining these economic disparities, we can better comprehend the far-reaching consequences of the caste system on individuals and society as a whole.

Conclusion:

In conclusion, this subchapter aims to provide sociologists with a comprehensive exploration of the Indian caste system and its multi-faceted impact. By examining its role in education, social inequality, intersectionality, history, economics, religion, politics, resistance movements, globalization, and international perspectives, we hope to foster a deeper understanding of this complex issue. Through this knowledge, we can work towards dismantling the caste system and creating a more inclusive and equitable society.

Chapter 1: The Impact of the Indian Caste System on Access to Education

Historical Background of Education in India

Education has played a significant role in the perpetuation of social inequality in India, with the Indian caste system being a central factor that determines access to education. To understand the current state of education in India, it is crucial to examine its historical background and the role of the caste system in shaping educational opportunities.

The origins of the Indian caste system can be traced back to ancient times, with the caste hierarchy being deeply rooted in Hindu religious texts. Originally, the caste system was intended to be a division of labor, with each caste having specific roles and responsibilities. However, over time, it morphed into a hereditary system of social stratification, where individuals were assigned a caste at birth, with limited mobility between castes.

Historically, education in India was primarily reserved for the upper castes, particularly the Brahmins, who had access to knowledge and were responsible for its transmission. The education system was designed to perpetuate social inequality by denying education to lower castes, such as the Dalits (formerly known as untouchables) and other marginalized communities.

During British colonial rule, the education system underwent significant changes. The British introduced modern education, which aimed to create a class of Indians educated in Western knowledge and values. However, this system also favored the upper castes, as they were more likely to have the financial resources and social capital to benefit from the new educational opportunities.

After independence, the Indian government took steps to address educational inequality. The constitution guaranteed the right to education for all citizens and implemented affirmative action policies, such as reservation quotas for Scheduled Castes and Scheduled Tribes in educational institutions. However, despite these efforts, access to quality education remains unequal, with lower castes and marginalized communities still facing numerous barriers.

The historical background of education in India provides a context for understanding the impact of the caste system on access to education and the perpetuation of social inequality. It highlights the need for sociologists to examine the intersectionality of caste, gender, and other social identities in understanding the experiences of women and marginalized communities in the education system.

Furthermore, studying the economic consequences of the caste system on different social classes is essential for understanding the broader impact of educational inequality. This knowledge can inform discussions on caste-based politics and the influence of caste in Indian elections and governance.

Moreover, sociologists can also explore the resistance against the caste system, with Dalit empowerment movements seeking to challenge and dismantle caste-based discrimination in education and society. Additionally, examining the impact of globalization on the caste system and comparing it with other forms of discrimination globally can provide valuable insights into the complexities of caste-based inequality.

In conclusion, understanding the historical background of education in India is crucial for sociologists studying the impact of the caste system on access to education and its role in perpetuating social inequality. By examining the origins and evolution of the caste system, religious justifications, economic consequences, and resistance movements, sociologists can contribute to the discourse on caste-based discrimination and work towards a more equitable education system in India.

Caste-based Discrimination in Educational Institutions

Introduction:

Caste-based discrimination is a deeply rooted issue that continues to plague Indian society, affecting various spheres of life, including access to education. This subchapter aims to shed light on the pervasive nature of caste-based discrimination in educational institutions and its implications for marginalized communities. By examining the experiences of different social classes, women, and marginalized communities, we can better understand the role of the Indian caste system in perpetuating social inequality.

Understanding the Impact of the Indian Caste System on Access to Education:

The Indian caste system has historically created barriers to educational opportunities for marginalized communities. Discrimination based on caste identity often leads to limited access to quality education, lower enrollment rates, and higher dropout rates among marginalized groups. The impact of the caste system on educational attainment contributes to the perpetuation of social inequality and the widening of the gap between privileged and disadvantaged groups.

Examining Intersectionality within the Indian Caste System:

Intersectionality plays a crucial role in understanding the experiences of women and marginalized communities within the Indian caste system. Women from lower castes face compounded discrimination, further limiting their access to education. This subchapter explores the unique challenges faced by these individuals and analyzes the intersection of gender and caste-based discrimination within educational institutions.

Historical Origins and Evolution of the Indian Caste System:

To comprehend the caste-based discrimination prevalent in educational institutions, it is essential to delve into the historical origins and evolution of the Indian caste system. This subchapter provides an overview of the caste system's historical context, tracing its development from ancient times to the present day. Understanding the roots of the caste system helps in identifying the deep-seated biases that contribute to the perpetuation of caste-based discrimination in education.

Economic Consequences of the Indian Caste System:

The economic consequences of the caste system on different social classes are significant. This subchapter explores how the caste system perpetuates economic inequality by limiting access to educational opportunities for marginalized communities. It also examines the impact of this inequality on social mobility and economic development in India.

Religious Justifications and Interpretations of the Indian Caste System:

Religion often plays a significant role in perpetuating the Indian caste system. This subchapter delves into the religious justifications and interpretations that support and reinforce caste-based discrimination. By examining religious beliefs and practices, we gain insight into the underlying ideologies that sustain the caste system and hinder progress towards a more egalitarian society.

Conclusion:

Caste-based discrimination in educational institutions is a pressing issue that demands attention from sociologists and policymakers alike. By exploring the impact of the Indian caste system on access to education, analyzing the experiences of marginalized communities, and examining its historical origins and economic consequences, we can begin to challenge and dismantle the systemic inequalities perpetuated by the caste system. Furthermore, international perspectives on the Indian caste system and comparisons with other forms of discrimination offer valuable insights for addressing this issue on a global scale. It is only through a comprehensive understanding of caste-based discrimination in educational institutions that we can work towards a more inclusive and equitable society for all.

Barriers to Education for Lower Caste Individuals

Introduction:

The Indian caste system is a deeply entrenched social structure that has been perpetuating inequality for centuries. One of the most significant consequences of this system is the barriers it creates for lower caste individuals in accessing education. This subchapter aims to explore the various obstacles faced by lower caste individuals in their pursuit of education, shedding light on the role of the caste system in perpetuating social inequality.

Historical Origins and Evolution:

To understand the barriers faced by lower caste individuals in education, it is essential to trace the historical origins and evolution of the Indian caste system. Starting as a division of labor, the caste system gradually developed into a rigid hierarchical structure, with the Brahmins at the top and the Dalits or lower castes at the bottom. This hierarchy has severely impacted educational opportunities for lower caste individuals throughout history.

Intersectionality and Experiences of Women and Marginalized Communities:

Examining the intersectionality of caste and gender is crucial to understanding the experiences of lower caste women in accessing education. These women face multiple layers of discrimination and often bear the brunt of caste-based educational barriers. Exploring their experiences helps highlight the urgent need for gender-sensitive policies and interventions.

Economic Consequences and Access to Education:

The economic consequences of the caste system play a significant role in limiting educational opportunities for lower caste individuals. Poverty, lack of resources, and limited access to quality education perpetuate the cycle of inequality. This subchapter will delve into the economic dimensions of caste-based educational barriers and their impact on different social classes.

Religious Justifications and Interpretations:

Religious justifications and interpretations of the caste system have further entrenched its influence on education. Certain religious texts and customs have been used to justify the unequal treatment of lower castes, including their exclusion from educational institutions. By examining these religious justifications, we can gain a deeper understanding of the caste system's resilience.

Dalit Empowerment Movements and Resistance:

Despite the numerous barriers they face, lower caste individuals have not been passive recipients of discrimination. Dalit empowerment movements and resistance against the caste system have emerged, advocating for equal educational opportunities. This subchapter will explore the strategies and successes of these movements, shedding light on the potential for change.

Conclusion:

The barriers to education faced by lower caste individuals are a significant manifestation of the Indian caste system's impact on perpetuating social inequality. By understanding these barriers and their historical, economic, and religious underpinnings, sociologists can contribute to the development of more inclusive policies and interventions. Addressing these barriers is crucial for breaking the cycle of inequality and creating a more equitable society. Additionally, international perspectives on the Indian caste system and comparisons with other forms of discrimination can provide valuable insights into the global fight against inequality.

Affirmative Action Policies and their Effectiveness

Affirmative action policies have been implemented in various countries around the world to address historical injustices and promote social equality. In the context of the Indian caste system, these policies have aimed to counteract the discrimination and marginalization faced by lower caste individuals and communities. This subchapter will explore the effectiveness of affirmative action policies in challenging the deep-rooted inequality perpetuated by the Indian caste system.

To begin with, it is essential to acknowledge the complex nature of caste-based discrimination and its impact on access to education. Affirmative action policies have played a significant role in increasing educational opportunities for marginalized groups. By implementing reservation quotas in educational institutions, these policies have enabled individuals from lower castes to gain admission and pursue higher education. However, the effectiveness of such policies in ensuring long-term equality and breaking the cycle of social disadvantage needs to be critically examined.

Furthermore, intersectionality provides a valuable lens through which to analyze the experiences of women and other marginalized communities within the Indian caste system. Affirmative action policies have attempted to address the multiple forms of discrimination faced by these groups. However, the extent to which these policies have been successful in empowering women and dismantling gender and caste-based inequalities requires further exploration.

Understanding the historical origins and evolution of the Indian caste system is crucial for comprehending the effectiveness of affirmative action policies. By examining the economic consequences of the caste system on different social classes, it becomes evident that affirmative action policies have had a significant impact on redistributing resources and opportunities. However, questions arise regarding the sustainability and long-term impact of these policies, given the deeply entrenched social hierarchies perpetuated by the caste system.

Moreover, the influence of the Indian caste system on politics and governance cannot be overlooked. Caste-based politics have shaped the electoral landscape in India, and affirmative action policies have been used as a tool to mobilize voters from lower castes. Analyzing the impact of these policies on political representation and governance is crucial to understanding their effectiveness in challenging social inequality.

While affirmative action policies have undoubtedly played a role in empowering marginalized communities, it is essential to critically evaluate their effectiveness in light of globalization and international perspectives. Comparisons with other forms of discrimination can provide valuable insights into the strengths and limitations of affirmative action policies in addressing the unique challenges posed by the Indian caste system.

In conclusion, this subchapter highlights the complexity and multidimensional nature of affirmative action policies in the context of the Indian caste system. By examining their effectiveness in various domains, such as education, intersectionality, economics, politics, and international perspectives, sociologists can gain a comprehensive understanding of the role and impact of these policies in perpetuating or challenging social inequality.

Case Studies: Educational Disparities Across Castes

The Indian caste system, with its deep-rooted social hierarchies, has had a profound impact on access to education in the country. This subchapter delves into case studies that highlight the educational disparities across castes, shedding light on the role of the caste system in perpetuating social inequality.

One such case study examines the experiences of marginalized communities, particularly Dalits, who have historically been subjected to severe discrimination and exclusion from educational opportunities. Despite government initiatives aimed at promoting education for all, Dalit students continue to face numerous obstacles, including caste-based discrimination, verbal and physical abuse, and lack of access to quality education. This case study underscores the intersectionality between caste and gender, as Dalit women face even greater challenges in accessing education.

Another case study focuses on the economic consequences of the caste system on different social classes. It highlights how individuals from higher castes have better access to educational resources, leading to enhanced economic opportunities and social mobility. On the other hand, individuals from lower castes often find themselves trapped in a cycle of poverty due to limited access to education and employment opportunities.

Furthermore, this subchapter explores the impact of the caste system on the political landscape of India. Caste-based politics play a significant role in Indian elections and governance, with politicians often exploiting caste divisions for their own benefit. This case study analyzes how the caste system influences voting patterns, political representation, and policy-making processes, further perpetuating social inequalities.

Moreover, the subchapter includes case studies that highlight the resistance against the caste system and the empowerment movements led by Dalits. These movements aim to challenge and dismantle the caste-based social order, advocating for equal access to education and opportunities for all individuals irrespective of their caste. The case studies examine the strategies employed by these movements, their successes, and the challenges they face in their quest for social justice.

By examining these case studies, sociologists gain a comprehensive understanding of the intricate relationship between the caste system and educational disparities in India. The subchapter provides valuable insights into the historical origins and evolution of the caste system, the economic implications, religious justifications, and international perspectives on the Indian caste system. It serves as a vital resource for researchers and scholars interested in understanding and addressing the multifaceted impacts of the caste system on education and social inequality in India.

Chapter 2: The Role of the Indian Caste System in Perpetuating Social Inequality

Social Hierarchy and Caste-Based Discrimination

In this subchapter, we delve into the complex dynamics of social hierarchy and caste-based discrimination in India, exploring their profound impact on various aspects of society. Addressed to sociologists, we aim to shed light on the multifaceted dimensions of the Indian caste system and its implications for different communities and social classes.

One crucial area affected by the caste system is access to education. We analyze how caste-based discrimination hampers educational opportunities, perpetuating social inequality. By examining the barriers faced by marginalized communities, including Dalits and women, we provide insights into the intersectionality of caste and gender, revealing the unique challenges faced by these groups.

To understand the roots of the Indian caste system, we delve into its historical origins and evolution. By exploring its religious justifications and interpretations, we uncover the complex interplay between religion and social hierarchy, shedding light on the deep-seated beliefs that sustain the caste system.

Furthermore, we examine the economic consequences of the caste system on different social classes. By analyzing the disparities in wealth, employment opportunities, and social mobility, we highlight the perpetuation of social inequality and economic disadvantage faced by lower castes.

Caste-based politics is another crucial aspect we explore. By analyzing the influence of caste in Indian elections and governance, we reveal how caste-based identities shape political dynamics, leading to the marginalization of certain communities while empowering others.

Additionally, we examine the resistance against the Indian caste system, particularly the Dalit empowerment movements that have emerged to challenge the discriminatory practices and fight for social justice. Through these movements, we gain insights into the strategies employed and the progress made in dismantling the caste system.

In a globalized world, we analyze the impact of globalization on the Indian caste system. By exploring how modernization, urbanization, and globalization intersect with caste dynamics, we uncover the changing nature of caste-based discrimination in contemporary society.

Finally, we broaden our perspective by comparing the Indian caste system with other forms of discrimination worldwide. By examining international perspectives, we highlight similarities and differences, providing a broader context for understanding the unique challenges posed by the Indian caste system.

In conclusion, this subchapter aims to provide sociologists with a comprehensive understanding of social hierarchy and caste-based discrimination in India. By examining various dimensions, including education, social inequality, gender, politics, resistance movements, and globalization, we offer a nuanced analysis of the Indian caste system and its impact on society.

Inter-generational Transmission of Caste Status

The inter-generational transmission of caste status is a key aspect in understanding the perpetuation of social inequality within the Indian caste system. This subchapter aims to delve into the intricate dynamics of how caste status is inherited and passed down from one generation to the next, shedding light on the mechanisms through which social stratification is sustained.

Caste status, deeply entrenched in Indian society, is not only a marker of social identity but also a determinant of one's access to education, economic opportunities, and political power. Sociologists studying the impact of the Indian caste system on access to education have consistently found that individuals from lower castes face significant barriers in obtaining quality education. This perpetuates a cycle of inequality as education is a crucial factor in social mobility and breaking free from caste-based restrictions.

Moreover, the inter-generational transmission of caste status intersects with the experiences of women and marginalized communities. Women from lower castes often face multiple layers of discrimination, further entrenching their subordinate position in society. This subchapter will explore the intersectionality of caste and gender, highlighting the specific challenges faced by women and marginalized communities in breaking free from the shackles of caste hierarchy.

To comprehend the inter-generational transmission of caste status, it is essential to examine the historical origins and evolution of the Indian caste system. This will provide sociologists with a broader understanding of how caste divisions were established and how they have persisted over centuries. Additionally, religious justifications and interpretations of the caste system have played a crucial role in its perpetuation, shaping societal attitudes and norms.

Furthermore, the economic consequences of the caste system on different social classes cannot be overlooked. The subchapter will delve into the disparities in wealth, occupation, and economic opportunities among different castes, shedding light on how the caste system perpetuates economic inequality.

Finally, international perspectives on the Indian caste system will be explored, drawing comparisons with other forms of discrimination. This will enable sociologists to gain insights from global experiences and foster a more nuanced understanding of the Indian caste system within a broader context.

In conclusion, the subchapter on the inter-generational transmission of caste status provides sociologists with a comprehensive analysis of how the Indian caste system perpetuates social inequality. By examining the impact on education, intersectionality, historical origins, economic consequences, religious justifications, and international perspectives, this subchapter offers a multifaceted exploration of the complexities surrounding the inter-generational transmission of caste status. Understanding these dynamics is crucial in formulating strategies to address and dismantle the barriers imposed by the caste system, ultimately working towards a more equitable and inclusive society.

Economic Disparities Among Castes

The Indian caste system is a complex social structure that has played a significant role in perpetuating social inequality and economic disparities among different castes. This subchapter will delve into the economic consequences of the Indian caste system on different social classes, shedding light on the challenges faced by marginalized communities and the implications for India's development.

The Indian caste system has deeply entrenched economic disparities. Historically, certain castes have been assigned to occupations that are considered low in social hierarchy, such as manual scavenging, leatherwork, or street cleaning. These occupations are often associated with low wages, poor working conditions, and limited opportunities for social mobility. As a result, individuals belonging to these castes are more likely to face poverty, unemployment, and lack of access to basic resources and services.

The impact of the caste system on access to education further exacerbates economic disparities. Discrimination and prejudice against lower castes often lead to limited educational opportunities for individuals from marginalized communities. This lack of education perpetuates the cycle of poverty and hinders social mobility, reinforcing the economic divide between different castes.

Furthermore, the role of the caste system in perpetuating social inequality intersects with gender, as women from marginalized castes face multiple forms of discrimination. They often bear the brunt of economic disparities, experiencing lower wages, limited job opportunities, and higher rates of poverty. Examining the experiences of women within the caste system provides valuable insights into the intersectionality of caste and gender and its impact on economic disparities.

Religious justifications and interpretations of the caste system have also contributed to economic disparities. The hierarchical nature of the caste system is often justified through religious beliefs, which reinforces the social and economic status quo. Religious practices and customs have historically limited the economic opportunities available to lower castes, making it difficult for them to break free from the cycle of poverty and discrimination.

Caste-based politics have played a significant role in Indian elections and governance, further entrenching economic disparities. Caste-based vote banks and political mobilization based on caste identities have influenced policy-making and resource allocation, often neglecting the needs of marginalized communities. This perpetuates economic inequalities and hinders the development of a more equitable society.

However, resistance against the Indian caste system has also emerged through Dalit empowerment movements. These movements aim to challenge the social and economic hierarchies by demanding equal rights, opportunities, and representation for marginalized castes. These movements have played a crucial role in raising awareness about the economic consequences of the caste system and advocating for social justice and equality.

In the context of globalization, the Indian caste system continues to have significant implications for economic disparities. Globalization has brought new economic opportunities, but it has also widened the gap between different castes. The marginalized castes often lack the resources and skills necessary to compete in the global market, further marginalizing them economically.

Finally, exploring international perspectives on the Indian caste system allows for comparisons with other forms of discrimination. By examining how other societies have addressed similar issues, we can gain insights into potential strategies for reducing economic disparities and promoting social equality within the Indian context.

In conclusion, economic disparities among castes are a critical aspect of the Indian caste system. Understanding the economic consequences of the caste system is essential for sociologists and researchers interested in studying the impact of the caste system on access to education, social inequality, intersectionality, and the experiences of marginalized communities. By examining the historical origins, religious justifications, and resistance movements against the caste system, we can gain a comprehensive understanding of the economic dimensions of this complex social structure. Furthermore, analyzing the economic implications of the caste system within the context of globalization and international comparisons provides valuable insights for addressing economic disparities and promoting social justice in India.

Social Exclusion and Stigmatization

Title: Social Exclusion and Stigmatization: Understanding the Impacts of the Indian Caste System

Introduction:

In this subchapter, we delve into the intricate dynamics of social exclusion and stigmatization within the Indian caste system. With a focus on the experiences of marginalized communities and women, we explore the historical origins, economic consequences, religious justifications, and contemporary implications of this deeply entrenched social structure. By examining the intersectionality of caste with education, social inequality, politics, globalization, and international perspectives, we aim to shed light on the multifaceted nature of the Indian caste system and its perpetuation of inequality.

Understanding the Impact on Access to Education:

One of the most significant consequences of the caste system is its adverse impact on access to education. We analyze how caste-based discrimination limits educational opportunities for marginalized communities, contributing to a cycle of poverty and social inequality. By examining the historical context and contemporary challenges, we highlight the urgent need for inclusive policies and interventions that address this issue.

The Role in Perpetuating Social Inequality:

The Indian caste system plays a pivotal role in perpetuating social inequality. We explore how caste-based discrimination permeates various aspects of life, including employment, housing, and social interactions. By examining the structural barriers faced by marginalized communities, we aim to deepen sociologists' understanding of the complex mechanisms through which social inequality is reinforced.

Intersectionality and Experiences of Women and Marginalized Communities:

An intersectional analysis of the Indian caste system is essential to comprehend the unique challenges faced by women and other marginalized communities. We explore how gender, class, and caste intersect to shape their experiences of social exclusion and stigmatization. By highlighting their voices and resistance movements, we aim to challenge the deeply entrenched norms and practices that perpetuate inequality.

Historical Origins and Evolution:

To understand the present-day implications of the caste system, we provide an overview of its historical origins and evolution. By examining its roots in ancient scriptures and the impact of colonization, we aim to contextualize the complex dynamics of the caste system and its transformation over time.

Economic Consequences on Different Social Classes:

The caste system has far-reaching economic consequences, affecting individuals from different social classes. We analyze how caste-based discrimination impacts economic opportunities, wealth distribution, and social mobility. By exploring the economic dimensions of the caste system, we aim to stimulate discussions on inclusive economic policies and strategies.

Religious Justifications and Interpretations:

Religious justifications and interpretations play a crucial role in perpetuating the caste system. We examine how religious beliefs and practices have been used to legitimize and reinforce social hierarchies. By critically analyzing these religious justifications, we aim to challenge the normative foundations of the caste system.

Caste-based Politics and Governance:

Caste-based politics has a profound influence on Indian elections and governance. We analyze the intricacies of caste-based voting patterns, the formation of caste-based political parties, and their impact on policymaking. By understanding the interplay between caste and politics, we aim to encourage sociologists to explore alternative modes of representation and governance.

Dalit Empowerment Movements and Resistance:

Dalit empowerment movements have emerged as powerful forces against the caste system. We examine the history, strategies, and achievements of these movements, highlighting their impact on challenging social exclusion and stigmatization. By showcasing their resilience and resistance, we aim to inspire sociologists to support and contribute to these transformative movements.

Globalization and the Indian Caste System:

Globalization has influenced the Indian caste system in various ways. We analyze the impacts of globalization on caste-based discrimination, economic opportunities, and social mobility. By exploring these dynamics, we aim to highlight the complexities of globalization and its interaction with the caste system.

International Perspectives and Comparisons with Other Forms of Discrimination:

Finally, we broaden the discussion by exploring international perspectives and comparing the Indian caste system with other forms of discrimination. By examining similarities and differences, we aim to foster dialogue and knowledge exchange among sociologists across different cultural contexts.

Conclusion:

This subchapter offers a comprehensive exploration of social exclusion and stigmatization within the Indian caste system. By addressing various themes and perspectives, we aim to deepen sociologists' understanding of the complex dynamics, implications, and resistance against this deeply entrenched social structure. Through critical analysis and interdisciplinary approaches, we hope to contribute to the ongoing efforts to combat inequality and foster inclusive societies.

Impact of Caste on Social Mobility

The Indian caste system has long been recognized as a significant barrier to social mobility, perpetuating inequality in numerous ways. This subchapter explores the profound impact of caste on social mobility, shedding light on the challenges faced by individuals and communities trying to transcend their assigned social status.

One of the key dimensions in which the caste system hampers social mobility is access to education. Historically, educational opportunities have been disproportionately distributed among different castes, with higher castes enjoying better access to quality education. This unequal access to education has resulted in a significant knowledge gap, limiting the upward mobility of lower-caste individuals and reinforcing the entrenched social hierarchy.

Furthermore, the role of the caste system in perpetuating social inequality cannot be overstated. Caste-based discrimination and prejudice continue to shape various aspects of Indian society, including employment opportunities, housing, and social interactions. Individuals from lower castes often face discrimination in the job market, leading to restricted career prospects and limited upward mobility. The inherent bias in the system ensures that social inequality is reproduced across generations, further entrenching the caste-based hierarchy.

The impact of caste on social mobility is not uniform and intersects with other forms of discrimination. Women, in particular, face compounded challenges due to their gender and caste identity. They are often subjected to multiple layers of discrimination and are further marginalized within their own communities. Similarly, other marginalized communities, such as the Dalits, face immense hurdles in achieving social mobility, as they are subjected to systemic oppression and exclusion.

Understanding the historical origins and evolution of the Indian caste system is crucial in comprehending its impact on social mobility. The system has deep roots in the ancient Indian society and has evolved over centuries, adapting to changing socio-political dynamics. Exploring these historical factors can provide valuable insights into the structural inequalities that persist today.

The economic consequences of the caste system are also significant. Different social classes are affected differently, with lower castes often occupying the lowest rungs of the economic ladder. Limited access to resources and opportunities, combined with discrimination, traps individuals in a cycle of poverty, hindering their social mobility.

Religious justifications and interpretations of the caste system have played a pivotal role in maintaining its legitimacy. These justifications have perpetuated the belief that social inequality is divinely ordained, making it challenging to challenge the system and its impact on social mobility.

Furthermore, the influence of caste in Indian politics and governance cannot be undermined. Caste-based politics significantly shapes elections and governance, further entrenching caste divisions and hindering social mobility.

However, there have been movements and resistance against the caste system, particularly led by Dalit empowerment movements. These movements have fought for the rights and social upliftment of marginalized communities, challenging the caste-based hierarchy and providing hope for increased social mobility.

The impact of globalization on the Indian caste system is also noteworthy. Globalization has both positive and negative consequences, providing opportunities for some individuals to break free from the constraints of the caste system while also exacerbating inequality in certain instances.

Lastly, international perspectives on the Indian caste system offer valuable comparisons with other forms of discrimination, shedding light on the universality of social hierarchies and the struggles faced by marginalized communities worldwide.

In summary, the impact of the caste system on social mobility is far-reaching and multifaceted. It affects access to education, perpetuates social inequality, intersects with other forms of discrimination, has deep historical roots, has economic consequences, is justified through religion, influences politics, and has faced resistance. Understanding and addressing these issues are crucial steps towards dismantling the caste-based hierarchy and promoting social mobility for all individuals, regardless of their caste identity.

Chapter 3: Intersectionality and the Indian Caste System: Examining the Experiences of Women and Marginalized Communities

Gender and Caste: Double Discrimination

In the complex social fabric of India, the intertwining forces of gender and caste have created a unique form of discrimination that impacts the lives of millions. This subchapter delves into the theme of "Gender and Caste: Double Discrimination," shedding light on the experiences of women and marginalized communities within the Indian caste system. It aims to provide sociologists with a deeper understanding of the challenges and complexities faced by these groups, and to explore the intersections between gender, caste, and social inequality.

The Indian caste system has long been criticized for its role in perpetuating social inequality. However, it is crucial to recognize that this inequality is not uniform; it is amplified by the additional layers of discrimination faced by women and marginalized communities. Women from lower castes often experience a double marginalization, as they grapple with both gender-based discrimination and caste-based oppression. This double discrimination has far-reaching consequences, particularly in terms of access to education and economic opportunities.

One of the key areas where the impact of the Indian caste system on access to education is evident is in the experiences of women. Discrimination based on both caste and gender limits their educational opportunities, perpetuating a cycle of inequality. Women from marginalized communities face multiple barriers, including limited resources, social stigma, and lack of representation in educational institutions.

Intersectionality provides a lens through which we can examine the unique experiences of women and marginalized communities within the Indian caste system. By understanding how different forms of discrimination intersect, we can gain a more comprehensive understanding of the challenges faced by these groups. This perspective helps us recognize the need for targeted interventions that address the specific needs and rights of these communities.

The historical origins and evolution of the Indian caste system are key to understanding its intersection with gender. The system's religious justifications and interpretations have perpetuated discriminatory practices, particularly against women and marginalized communities. Additionally, caste-based politics have played a significant role in Indian elections and governance, shaping policies that either perpetuate or challenge the existing social hierarchy.

Despite the immense challenges, there have been Dalit empowerment movements and resistance against the Indian caste system. These movements have sought to challenge the deeply entrenched discrimination faced by marginalized communities and have worked towards empowering women within these communities.

The impact of globalization on the Indian caste system is also worth exploring. While globalization has brought economic growth and opportunities, it has also exacerbated existing inequalities, including those based on caste and gender. Understanding these dynamics is crucial for sociologists seeking to analyze the broader implications of globalization on social structures.

Finally, this subchapter offers international perspectives on the Indian caste system, drawing comparisons with other forms of discrimination.

By examining caste in a global context, we can identify commonalities and differences with other systems of oppression, helping us develop a more nuanced understanding of the issues at hand.

In conclusion, this subchapter delves into the intricate relationship between gender and caste, shedding light on the experiences of women and marginalized communities within the Indian caste system. By examining the impact of caste on access to education, perpetuation of social inequality, and the experiences of different social classes, we gain a deeper understanding of the complexities of this system. Through intersectional analysis, historical perspectives, and international comparisons, we can shape a more comprehensive understanding of the Indian caste system and its role in perpetuating inequality.

Caste-Based Violence Against Women

Caste-based violence against women is a deeply rooted issue in Indian society, perpetuating the inequalities inherent in the caste system. This subchapter delves into the various forms of violence faced by women belonging to different castes, highlighting the intersectionality of gender, caste, and other marginalized identities.

One of the key aspects explored in this subchapter is the impact of the Indian caste system on access to education for women. It is well-documented that women from lower castes face significant barriers to education, which limits their social mobility and perpetuates the cycle of inequality. The subchapter discusses the specific challenges faced by women from marginalized castes in accessing quality education and the long-term consequences this has on their empowerment.

Furthermore, this subchapter delves into the role of the Indian caste system in perpetuating social inequality, particularly in relation to women. It explores how caste-based discrimination intersects with gender discrimination, resulting in compounded disadvantages for women from lower castes. The subchapter examines the ways in which the caste system reinforces patriarchal norms and restricts opportunities for women, exacerbating gender-based violence and discrimination.

Drawing on historical perspectives, the subchapter also explores the origins and evolution of the Indian caste system. It traces the roots of caste-based violence against women and how it has evolved over time, shedding light on the intergenerational transmission of caste-based discrimination and violence.

Additionally, the subchapter addresses the economic consequences of the Indian caste system on different social classes, examining how caste-based violence against women further marginalizes them economically. It highlights the link between caste-based violence and poverty, as women from lower castes are often denied economic opportunities and subjected to exploitative labor practices.

Finally, this subchapter delves into the resistance against the Indian caste system, focusing on Dalit empowerment movements. It explores the strategies employed by marginalized communities and women to challenge caste-based violence and discrimination, shedding light on the resilience and agency of those affected.

In conclusion, this subchapter offers sociologists a comprehensive understanding of caste-based violence against women in India. It highlights the need for intersectional analysis to comprehend the complex dynamics at play and calls for further research and action to dismantle the structures that perpetuate such violence and inequality.

Caste and Intersectionality with Religion, Language, and Disability

In the complex web of social hierarchies that is the Indian caste system, various factors intersect to shape individuals' experiences and perpetuate inequality. This subchapter explores the intersections of caste with religion, language, and disability, shedding light on the nuanced ways in which these dimensions interact and contribute to social discrimination and marginalization.

Religion plays a significant role in the Indian caste system, often serving as a basis for legitimizing and perpetuating social stratification. Religious justifications and interpretations of the caste system have historically reinforced the hierarchical structure, with certain castes considered "pure" and others deemed "impure" or "untouchable." These religious beliefs and practices have had far-reaching implications, influencing social interactions, access to resources, and opportunities for upward mobility.

Language is another important aspect of caste intersectionality. Different castes have historically been associated with specific languages, leading to linguistic divisions and inequalities. Language-based discrimination can be seen in educational institutions, employment opportunities, and social interactions, further entrenching caste-based hierarchies. The impact of language on social mobility and access to education is particularly pronounced, with marginalized castes often facing barriers to quality education due to language-based discrimination.

Disability intersects with caste to create additional layers of marginalization and exclusion. Marginalized castes often have limited access to healthcare and support systems, exacerbating the challenges faced by individuals with disabilities. Discrimination against individuals with disabilities is compounded by caste-based prejudice, leading to increased social isolation and limited opportunities for economic empowerment.

Understanding the intersections of caste with religion, language, and disability is crucial for sociologists researching the Indian caste system.

By examining these intersections, researchers can gain deeper insights into the complexities and mechanisms through which caste-based discrimination is perpetuated. This knowledge can inform interventions aimed at dismantling the caste system, promoting social equality, and empowering marginalized communities.

Moreover, examining the intersections of caste with other forms of discrimination, such as gender and class, can provide a comprehensive understanding of the multiple dimensions of inequality experienced by women and marginalized communities in India. This intersectional perspective highlights the unique challenges faced by individuals at the intersections of multiple marginalized identities and emphasizes the need for inclusive policies and social justice movements that address these intersecting inequalities.

By exploring the intersections of caste with religion, language, and disability, this subchapter contributes to the broader discourse on the Indian caste system's impact on social inequality. It provides sociologists with a comprehensive understanding of the complexities and interplay of various dimensions of marginalization, paving the way for informed interventions and advocacy efforts to dismantle this deeply entrenched system of oppression.

Marginalized Communities and Caste: A Subjugated Existence

In the vast landscape of Indian society, the Indian caste system has played a significant role in perpetuating social inequality and marginalizing certain communities. This subchapter aims to shed light on the subjugated existence experienced by marginalized communities, focusing on the impact of the Indian caste system.

One crucial aspect to explore is the impact of the caste system on access to education. Historically, certain castes have been denied the right to education, leading to severe disparities in literacy rates and educational opportunities. This perpetuates social inequality as education is often seen as a pathway to social mobility and economic well-being.

Furthermore, the intersectionality between gender and caste is another critical lens through which to examine the experiences of marginalized communities. Women belonging to lower castes face a double marginalization, experiencing gender discrimination alongside caste-based oppression. This intersectionality exacerbates the challenges faced by these women, limiting their opportunities for empowerment and social progress.

To understand the roots of this system, it is imperative to delve into the historical origins and evolution of the Indian caste system. By examining its origins, we can better comprehend how it has solidified and entrenched social hierarchies over centuries, resulting in the present-day realities faced by marginalized communities.

The economic consequences of the caste system on different social classes also warrant discussion. The system has created a deeply entrenched division of labor, where certain castes are confined to menial and low-paying jobs, while higher castes dominate positions of power and privilege. This economic disparity further reinforces social inequality and perpetuates the subjugated existence of marginalized communities.

Religious justifications and interpretations of the caste system have also played a significant role in its perpetuation. Examining these religious beliefs and practices can provide insights into the mindset and social acceptance of the caste system, despite its oppressive nature.

Caste-based politics is another crucial aspect to analyze. The influence of caste in Indian elections and governance has shaped political landscapes, leading to a deeply entrenched system of representation that often fails to address the needs and concerns of marginalized communities.

However, resistance against the Indian caste system is not absent. Dalit empowerment movements have emerged, challenging the discriminatory practices and advocating for equal rights and opportunities. Understanding these movements and their impact is essential in developing strategies to dismantle the caste system and uplift marginalized communities.

In the context of globalization, it is essential to examine the impact of global forces on the Indian caste system. Globalization has brought both challenges and opportunities for marginalized communities, and understanding these dynamics is crucial in addressing their subjugated existence.

Lastly, international perspectives on the Indian caste system can provide valuable insights. Comparisons with other forms of discrimination can help sociologists and scholars understand the unique characteristics of the Indian caste system and its implications for social inequality.

By exploring the subjugated existence of marginalized communities within the Indian caste system, this subchapter aims to contribute to the ongoing dialogue on social inequality and prompt sociologists to critically examine the complexities and nuances of the caste system. Only through a comprehensive understanding can we hope to challenge and dismantle the barriers that perpetuate inequality in Indian society.

Resistance and Empowerment of Women and Marginalized Communities

In exploring the role of the Indian caste system, it is crucial to examine the resistance and empowerment of women and marginalized communities. The Indian caste system has long perpetuated social inequality, denying access to education and opportunities for those at the bottom of the social hierarchy. This subchapter delves into the experiences of these individuals, highlighting their struggles, resilience, and the movements that have emerged to challenge the caste system.

The impact of the Indian caste system on access to education has been profound. Historically, lower castes and marginalized communities have faced discrimination and exclusion from educational institutions. This subchapter sheds light on the barriers they encounter, such as limited resources, biased curriculum, and societal prejudices, which hinder their educational development. It also explores the efforts made by activists and organizations to bridge this gap and create equal educational opportunities for all.

Furthermore, intersectionality plays a significant role in understanding the experiences of women and marginalized communities within the caste system. This subchapter examines the unique challenges faced by Dalit women, Adivasis, and other marginalized groups, who experience multiple forms of discrimination based on their gender, caste, and economic status. It highlights their resilience, agency, and the strategies they employ to challenge and navigate these intersecting oppressions.

The historical origins and evolution of the Indian caste system are also explored, providing a context for understanding its impact on different social classes. By examining the economic consequences of the caste system, this subchapter reveals how it perpetuates social inequality, with certain castes enjoying privilege and power while others are trapped in cycles of poverty and exploitation.

Religious justifications and interpretations of the caste system are also critically examined. The subchapter delves into the religious texts and practices that have perpetuated and justified caste-based discrimination, while also highlighting alternative interpretations that challenge these oppressive beliefs.

Moreover, this subchapter addresses the role of caste in Indian politics and governance. It analyzes the influence of caste in elections and the formation of government, shedding light on the ways in which caste-based politics perpetuate inequality and shape policies that either uplift or further marginalize certain communities.

Finally, the subchapter discusses the resistance movements and empowerment initiatives that have emerged to challenge the Indian caste system. It explores the Dalit empowerment movements, feminist organizations, and other grassroots efforts that seek to dismantle caste-based discrimination and create a more equitable society.

By examining the resistance and empowerment of women and marginalized communities within the Indian caste system, this subchapter provides valuable insights for sociologists studying the impact of the caste system on education, social inequality, and the experiences of various communities. It also offers a broader understanding of the Indian caste system in comparison to other forms of discrimination, both within India and internationally.

Chapter 4: The Historical Origins and Evolution of the Indian Caste System

Ancient Indian Society and the Varna System

The Varna system, an ancient social structure that divided Indian society into distinct classes, has played a significant role in shaping the country's history and perpetuating social inequality. To truly understand the impact of the Indian caste system, it is crucial to delve into its historical origins and evolution.

The Varna system originated in ancient India, where society was divided into four main varnas or classes: the Brahmins (priests and scholars), Kshatriyas (warriors and rulers), Vaishyas (merchants and farmers), and Shudras (laborers and servants). Each varna had specific roles and responsibilities within society, and individuals were born into their respective varna, determined by their family lineage.

The Varna system was initially intended to organize society based on individuals' skills and aptitudes. However, over time, it transformed into a rigid social hierarchy, where birth determined one's social status and opportunities. This hierarchical structure perpetuated social inequality, as individuals from lower castes were systematically marginalized and denied access to education, economic opportunities, and political power.

The impact of the Indian caste system on access to education has been profound. Members of lower castes, especially Dalits, also known as untouchables, faced discrimination and exclusion from educational institutions. This denied them the chance to acquire knowledge and skills necessary for social mobility, perpetuating their marginalization and reinforcing social inequality.

Furthermore, the Indian caste system intersected with gender and marginalized communities, intensifying the discrimination faced by women and other marginalized groups. Women from lower castes experienced multiple layers of oppression, as they faced discrimination not only based on their gender but also their caste. This intersectionality further limited their access to education, healthcare, and economic opportunities.

Religious justifications and interpretations have been used to justify the Indian caste system throughout history. Some religious texts and beliefs propagated the idea that individuals are born into their caste as a result of their past actions in previous lives. This religious legitimization of the caste system has made it deeply embedded in Indian society and resistant to change.

Dalit empowerment movements have emerged as a response to the injustices perpetuated by the caste system. These movements aim to challenge social norms, demand equal rights and opportunities, and raise awareness about the discrimination faced by Dalits. These movements have played a vital role in advocating for social justice and equality.

In recent years, globalization has also had an impact on the Indian caste system. While globalization has brought economic growth and opportunities, it has also widened the gap between different social classes. The upper castes have been able to benefit from globalization, while the lower castes continue to face discrimination and limited economic mobility.

Understanding the Indian caste system in an international context is crucial. Comparisons with other forms of discrimination can provide valuable insights into the complexities of social hierarchies and the challenges faced by marginalized communities worldwide.

In conclusion, the Varna system is an integral part of ancient Indian society and has influenced the country's social structure for centuries. The caste system has perpetuated social inequality, hindered access to education, and marginalized women and other marginalized communities. It is essential for sociologists to explore the historical origins, economic consequences, religious justifications, and resistance movements associated with the Indian caste system to understand its impact on society and work towards creating a more equal and inclusive future.

Influence of Religion on the Caste System

Religion plays a significant role in shaping and perpetuating the Indian caste system, a complex social structure that has endured for centuries. The interplay between religion and caste has profound implications for various aspects of society, including access to education, social inequality, gender dynamics, economic disparities, politics, resistance movements, and even global perspectives on discrimination. This subchapter aims to shed light on the influence of religion on the caste system, highlighting its multifaceted nature and exploring its implications for sociologists and scholars interested in understanding this pervasive social phenomenon.

Religious justifications and interpretations form the bedrock of the Indian caste system. The Hindu religion, with its beliefs in karma and dharma, provides a moral and spiritual framework that has been used to legitimize the hierarchical division of society. The idea of varna, or the four-fold social order, assigns individuals to specific castes based on their perceived inherent qualities and occupations. This religious sanction has contributed to the social acceptance and perpetuation of the caste system, making it deeply ingrained in Indian society.

Furthermore, religion intersects with gender and marginalization, resulting in unique experiences for women and marginalized communities within the caste system. Women often face double oppression due to their gender and caste, experiencing discrimination and limited opportunities in education, employment, and social mobility. Understanding the intersectionality of caste and gender within a religious context is crucial for addressing the specific challenges faced by these communities.

Religion also plays a role in caste-based politics and governance. Caste-based political parties have emerged, representing the interests of specific castes and mobilizing their support during elections. This has had a significant impact on the political landscape, shaping policies and perpetuating social divisions. Sociologists studying caste-based politics must delve into the religious dimensions that underpin and motivate these movements.

Resistance against the caste system has also been driven by religious empowerment movements. Dalit communities, historically oppressed and marginalized, have organized themselves to challenge the caste hierarchy and demand social justice. These movements draw on religious narratives and reinterpretations to assert their rights and challenge the religious justifications used to perpetuate inequality.

An examination of the influence of religion on the caste system requires a global perspective as well. Comparisons can be drawn with other forms of discrimination and social hierarchies, allowing for a deeper understanding of the Indian caste system's unique characteristics and its broader implications for societies grappling with inequality.

In conclusion, the influence of religion on the Indian caste system is extensive and multifaceted. Its impact can be observed in various spheres, including education, social inequality, gender dynamics, economics, politics, resistance movements, and global perspectives. By exploring the religious justifications and interpretations that underpin the caste system, sociologists can gain valuable insights into the complexities of this social structure and work towards dismantling its perpetuation of inequality.

Changes and Adaptations in the Caste System over Time

The Indian caste system is a complex social structure that has evolved and changed over centuries, shaping the lives of millions of people in India. In this subchapter, we will explore the various changes and adaptations that have taken place within the caste system over time, shedding light on the dynamics of social hierarchy and inequality in Indian society.

One significant change in the caste system has been its impact on access to education. Historically, the caste system has limited educational opportunities for lower castes, perpetuating social inequality. However, in recent years, there have been efforts to address this issue through affirmative action policies and reservations for marginalized communities. Sociologists have examined the effectiveness of these measures in promoting equal access to education and the challenges faced in implementation.

Furthermore, the role of the caste system in perpetuating social inequality has undergone changes as well. While the caste system was originally based on occupation and hereditary divisions, it has now become more entrenched in social, economic, and political spheres. Sociologists have explored how the caste system intersects with other forms of discrimination, particularly in the experiences of women and marginalized communities. This intersectionality has provided a nuanced understanding of the multiple layers of oppression faced by individuals in lower castes.

The historical origins and evolution of the caste system have also undergone significant changes. Initially, the system was fluid and

PERPETUATING INEQUALITY: EXPLORING THE ROLE OF THE INDIAN CASTE SYSTEM

allowed for social mobility. However, it became rigid and hierarchical over time, leading to the entrenchment of social inequalities. Sociologists have traced the historical developments that led to this transformation and analyzed the economic consequences of the caste system on different social classes.

Religious justifications and interpretations of the caste system have influenced its evolution as well. Sociologists have examined the religious texts and traditions that have reinforced the hierarchical structure of the caste system and explored alternative interpretations that challenge its discriminatory practices.

Caste-based politics and its influence on Indian elections and governance have also evolved over time. Sociologists have analyzed the role of caste in electoral politics and the impact it has on policy-making and representation. Additionally, the resistance against the caste system and the empowerment movements of Dalits have brought about significant changes in challenging caste-based discrimination.

The impact of globalization on the caste system has also been a topic of study for sociologists. They have explored how globalization has both challenged and reinforced the caste system, examining its effects on economic opportunities, social mobility, and cultural practices.

Lastly, international perspectives on the Indian caste system have provided comparative insights into other forms of discrimination. Sociologists have examined similarities and differences between the Indian caste system and other systems of social stratification, shedding light on the global dimensions of inequality.

In conclusion, this subchapter delves into the changes and adaptations that have occurred within the Indian caste system over time. By examining various aspects such as education, social inequality, intersectionality, historical origins, economic consequences, religious justifications, politics, resistance movements, globalization, and international perspectives, sociologists gain a comprehensive understanding of the complex dynamics surrounding the Indian caste system.

Caste System in Modern India: Continuity and Transformation

The Indian caste system has been a subject of immense interest and debate among sociologists, as it continues to shape the socio-economic and political landscape of modern India. This subchapter delves into the various aspects of the caste system, focusing on its continuity and transformation in contemporary times.

One crucial area of study is the impact of the caste system on access to education. Despite efforts to promote equality, the caste system still plays a significant role in determining educational opportunities for different social groups. This subchapter explores the barriers faced by marginalized communities, especially Dalits, and analyzes the ways in which the caste system perpetuates social inequality through unequal access to education.

Intersectionality is another important lens through which the Indian caste system can be examined. This subchapter aims to understand the experiences of women and other marginalized communities within the caste system. By exploring their unique challenges and discrimination, it sheds light on the complex interplay between gender, caste, and social inequality.

Understanding the historical origins and evolution of the caste system is crucial to comprehending its present manifestations. This subchapter provides a comprehensive overview of the caste system's historical development, tracing its roots to ancient times and examining the factors that have contributed to its persistence in modern India.

PERPETUATING INEQUALITY: EXPLORING THE ROLE OF THE INDIAN CASTE SYSTEM

The economic consequences of the caste system on different social classes are also explored in this subchapter. By analyzing the economic disparities among castes and the role of caste-based occupations, it highlights how the caste system perpetuates economic inequality and hinders social mobility.

Religious justifications and interpretations of the caste system are another significant aspect to be considered. This subchapter examines the religious texts and practices that have reinforced the caste system, shedding light on the religious underpinnings that have sustained its existence.

Furthermore, the influence of the caste system in Indian politics and governance is explored in detail. By analyzing caste-based politics and its impact on elections and policymaking, this subchapter reveals the intricate relationship between caste and political power in contemporary India.

The subchapter also highlights the resistance against the caste system through Dalit empowerment movements. By examining the strategies and achievements of these movements, it showcases the ongoing struggle against caste-based discrimination and the quest for social justice.

Globalization has undoubtedly influenced the caste system in various ways, and this subchapter explores its impact. By examining the changes brought about by globalization, such as increased mobility and exposure to diverse cultures, it highlights the challenges and opportunities that globalization presents for the caste system.

Lastly, this subchapter provides an international perspective on the Indian caste system, drawing comparisons with other forms of discrimination worldwide. By analyzing similarities and differences, it aims to broaden the understanding of the caste system and its significance in a global context.

Overall, this subchapter offers a comprehensive exploration of the caste system in modern India, addressing various dimensions such as education, social inequality, intersectionality, historical origins, economic consequences, religious justifications, politics, resistance, globalization, and international perspectives. It aims to provide sociologists with a nuanced understanding of the complexities surrounding the Indian caste system and its enduring impact on Indian society.

Comparison with Caste-Like Systems in Other Cultures

The Indian caste system has long been a subject of fascination and study for sociologists around the world. Its unique structure and impact on society make it a topic of great importance for understanding social inequality and discrimination. However, it is also valuable to explore the similarities and differences between the Indian caste system and similar systems in other cultures. By examining these comparisons, we can gain a broader perspective on the causes and consequences of such systems.

One example of a caste-like system in another culture is the Japanese Burakumin. Similar to the Indian caste system, the Burakumin are a marginalized group who face discrimination and social exclusion. They are often associated with occupations such as butchery and leatherwork, which are considered impure in Japanese society. This parallel with the Indian caste system highlights the universality of social hierarchies based on occupation and birth.

Another interesting comparison can be made with the apartheid system in South Africa. Although not strictly a caste system, apartheid was a racial segregation system that resulted in the marginalization of the black population. Like the Indian caste system, apartheid reinforced social inequality and limited access to education and opportunities for certain racial groups. This comparison demonstrates how discrimination and inequality can manifest in different ways in different societies.

Furthermore, examining the Roma people in Europe provides another perspective on caste-like systems. The Roma face widespread discrimination and prejudice across the continent. They are often relegated to the lowest socio-economic positions and suffer from limited access to education and healthcare. This comparison highlights the commonalities in the experiences of marginalized communities across different cultures.

Studying these and other caste-like systems in other cultures allows us to gain a more comprehensive understanding of the Indian caste system. By examining the historical origins, economic consequences, religious justifications, and political influences of these systems, we can identify patterns and dynamics that transcend cultural boundaries. This comparative approach helps to shed light on the underlying mechanisms that perpetuate social inequality and discrimination.

In conclusion, comparing the Indian caste system with caste-like systems in other cultures provides valuable insights into the causes and consequences of social hierarchies. Sociologists studying the impact of the Indian caste system on access to education, social inequality, intersectionality, and other related topics can benefit from a broader perspective that takes into account the similarities and differences with other forms of discrimination. By exploring these comparisons, we can continue to deepen our understanding of the Indian caste system and its implications for society as a whole.

Chapter 5: The Economic Consequences of the Indian Caste System on Different Social Classes

Caste-Based Occupational Segregation

Caste-based occupational segregation is a crucial aspect of the Indian caste system, which has been a major force in perpetuating social inequality in the country. This subchapter will delve into the various dimensions of this segregation, examining its historical origins, economic consequences, and impact on different social classes. Sociologists studying the impact of the Indian caste system on access to education, the role of the Indian caste system in perpetuating social inequality, and the experiences of marginalized communities and women will find this subchapter particularly insightful.

The Indian caste system has historically assigned occupations based on birth, leading to a rigid division of labor and limited social mobility. This subchapter will explore how this division has resulted in a stark disparity in access to education. Members of lower castes, particularly Dalits, have faced significant barriers in obtaining quality education, further perpetuating social inequality. By analyzing the role of the caste system in shaping educational opportunities, sociologists can better understand the mechanisms through which inequality is reproduced.

Moreover, this subchapter will shed light on the economic consequences of caste-based occupational segregation. The caste system has restricted certain occupations to specific castes, leading to unequal distribution of wealth and resources. By examining the economic implications of this segregation on different social classes, sociologists can gain a comprehensive understanding of the interplay between caste, occupation, and economic status.

Furthermore, this subchapter will explore the intersectionality of the Indian caste system, focusing on the experiences of women and marginalized communities. It will highlight how caste intersects with gender, class, and other forms of discrimination, resulting in compounded disadvantages. By examining these intersections, sociologists can gain insight into the unique challenges faced by different social groups and develop strategies to address them.

The subchapter will also touch upon the historical origins and evolution of the Indian caste system, religious justifications and interpretations, caste-based politics, and the impact of globalization on the caste system. Additionally, it will provide international perspectives on the Indian caste system, drawing comparisons with other forms of discrimination.

Overall, this subchapter aims to provide sociologists with a comprehensive analysis of caste-based occupational segregation and its implications. By understanding the complexities of the Indian caste system, sociologists can contribute to the development of policies and interventions that aim to reduce inequality and promote social justice in India.

Economic Exploitation and Wage Disparities

The Indian caste system is not only a social hierarchy but also a mechanism that perpetuates economic exploitation and wage disparities within Indian society. This subchapter aims to delve into the economic consequences of the caste system on different social classes, examining how it affects access to education, perpetuates social inequality, and disproportionately impacts women and marginalized communities.

Access to education is a fundamental factor in breaking the cycle of poverty and achieving social mobility. However, the caste system has created significant barriers in this regard. Historically, individuals from lower castes have been excluded from educational opportunities, resulting in limited skills and knowledge. This lack of education perpetuates their social and economic marginalization, trapping them in low-wage jobs and denying them the chance to improve their living conditions.

Moreover, the caste system reinforces social inequality by assigning certain occupations to specific castes. This occupational segregation limits the economic prospects of individuals from lower castes, as they are often confined to menial and low-paying jobs. Conversely, individuals from higher castes enjoy better access to education, leading to higher-paying jobs and greater social mobility.

The impact of the caste system is particularly harsh on women and marginalized communities. Women from lower castes face multiple layers of discrimination and exploitation, both within their own communities and in wider society. They are disproportionately affected by poverty, lack of access to education, and limited job opportunities, further entrenching their subordinate status.

Marginalized communities, such as the Dalits, face economic exploitation due to their low caste status. They are often subjected to bonded labor, where they are trapped in a cycle of debt and forced to work in deplorable conditions for minimal wages. This systemic exploitation is not only an infringement of their basic human rights but also perpetuates their economic vulnerability.

Understanding the economic consequences of the caste system is crucial for sociologists studying social inequality in India. By examining the intersectionality of caste, gender, and other marginalized identities, researchers can gain insights into the complex dynamics that perpetuate economic exploitation and wage disparities. This knowledge can inform policies and interventions aimed at dismantling the caste system's economic implications and promoting equal opportunities for all individuals, regardless of their caste or social background.

In conclusion, the Indian caste system has far-reaching economic consequences, perpetuating inequality and wage disparities across different social classes. By analyzing its impact on education, social mobility, and the experiences of women and marginalized communities, sociologists can deepen their understanding of the complex interplay between caste, economics, and social inequality. This knowledge is essential for addressing and dismantling the caste system's economic exploitations and working towards a more equitable society.

Entrepreneurship Opportunities and Caste-based Networks

In the complex social structure of India, entrepreneurship opportunities are intricately linked with caste-based networks. The Indian caste system, with its hierarchical division of society based on occupation and social status, plays a crucial role in shaping the entrepreneurial landscape of the country. Understanding the dynamics of caste-based networks and their impact on entrepreneurship is vital to comprehending the broader implications of the Indian caste system on economic development and social inequality.

Caste-based networks, formed through generations of social interaction and interdependence, serve as a foundation for entrepreneurship opportunities in India. Within these networks, individuals are provided with access to resources, knowledge, and social capital necessary for entrepreneurial success. These networks operate through a system of patronage, where individuals belonging to higher castes extend support and guidance to those from lower castes. This assistance includes financial aid, mentorship, and access to markets and customers. As a result, caste-based networks act as a gateway for aspiring entrepreneurs, particularly those from disadvantaged castes, to overcome barriers and establish their businesses.

However, the intricate link between entrepreneurship and caste-based networks also perpetuates social inequality. The Indian caste system, with its inherent stratification, limits access to entrepreneurship opportunities for marginalized communities. Historically disadvantaged castes, such as Dalits and other lower castes, face discrimination and exclusion from these networks. As a consequence, they are deprived of the resources and support necessary to start and sustain successful businesses. This perpetuates social inequality, as entrepreneurship is considered a pathway to economic mobility and upward social mobility.

Moreover, the intersectionality of caste and gender further compounds the challenges faced by women from marginalized communities in accessing entrepreneurship opportunities. Women belonging to lower castes encounter multiple forms of discrimination and face additional barriers due to patriarchal norms and practices. They often struggle to break free from the constraints imposed by both caste and gender, limiting their participation in entrepreneurial activities.

To address these issues, it is essential to critically examine the historical origins and evolution of the Indian caste system. By understanding its roots, we can better comprehend the economic consequences it has on different social classes and devise strategies to mitigate its negative impact. Additionally, religious justifications and interpretations of the caste system should be critically analyzed to challenge and debunk the prevailing beliefs that perpetuate discrimination.

Furthermore, policymakers and sociologists need to analyze the influence of caste in Indian elections and governance. Caste-based politics have significant implications for entrepreneurship opportunities, as political power often determines access to resources and government support. By scrutinizing the role of caste in these domains, we can work towards creating a more inclusive and equitable environment for entrepreneurship in India.

Dalit empowerment movements and resistance against the Indian caste system are also crucial in dismantling the barriers faced by marginalized communities. By advocating for equal rights and opportunities, these movements highlight the importance of eradicating caste-based discrimination and promoting social justice.

Lastly, examining the impact of globalization on the Indian caste system and comparing it with other forms of discrimination across the globe provides valuable insights into the broader phenomenon of social inequality. By understanding the unique challenges posed by the Indian caste system and its international implications, we can work towards developing strategies to address discrimination in a global context.

In conclusion, entrepreneurship opportunities in India are intricately linked to caste-based networks. While these networks offer advantages for some, they also perpetuate social inequality and limit access to marginalized communities. By critically examining the role of caste in entrepreneurship, understanding its historical origins, and promoting inclusive policies, we can strive for a more equitable society and create opportunities for all.

Caste and Poverty: Breaking the Cycle

The Indian caste system has long been a subject of interest and debate for sociologists, and one of the key aspects that cannot be ignored is its impact on poverty. In this subchapter, we will explore the intricate relationship between caste and poverty, and discuss potential strategies for breaking the cycle of inequality.

The Indian caste system has historically marginalized certain communities and perpetuated social inequality. This has had a profound impact on access to education, with marginalized groups facing significant barriers to quality education. As a result, poverty becomes a self-perpetuating cycle, as lack of education limits opportunities for economic advancement.

The intersectionality of caste and gender adds another layer of complexity to this issue. Women and marginalized communities within the caste system face compounded discrimination, leading to even greater levels of poverty and social exclusion. Understanding their experiences is crucial in developing effective interventions.

To fully comprehend the caste-poverty nexus, it is essential to examine the historical origins and evolution of the Indian caste system. This will shed light on how the system has been deeply ingrained in Indian society, affecting economic structures and perpetuating inequality.

The economic consequences of the caste system are far-reaching, with different social classes experiencing varying degrees of disadvantage. The upper castes tend to enjoy more economic privileges, while lower castes, particularly Dalits, often face extreme poverty and exploitation. This economic divide further entrenches social inequality and hampers overall development.

Religious justifications and interpretations of the caste system have also played a significant role in perpetuating its existence. Challenging these religious beliefs and promoting a more inclusive understanding of spirituality is crucial in dismantling the caste system and reducing poverty.

Moreover, the influence of caste in Indian politics and governance cannot be understated. Caste-based politics has shaped electoral dynamics and policy-making, often reinforcing caste divisions rather than alleviating poverty. Understanding these dynamics is essential for developing effective governance strategies.

However, there is hope. Dalit empowerment movements and resistance against the caste system have gained momentum in recent years. These movements aim to challenge discriminatory practices, raise awareness, and advocate for social justice. Supporting and amplifying these movements can be a step towards breaking the cycle of poverty and inequality.

The impact of globalization on the Indian caste system is another area of exploration. Globalization has both positive and negative consequences, with the potential to challenge traditional caste-based hierarchies while also exacerbating social disparities. Studying these dynamics will provide valuable insights into the future of the caste system.

Lastly, it is important to consider international perspectives on the Indian caste system. Comparing it with other forms of discrimination can help identify commonalities and unique aspects, leading to a more comprehensive understanding of caste-based inequality.

In conclusion, the relationship between caste and poverty is complex and deeply rooted in Indian society. Addressing this issue requires a multi-faceted approach, including educational reforms, empowering marginalized communities, challenging religious justifications, and supporting movements for social justice. By breaking the cycle of poverty perpetuated by the caste system, India can move towards a more equitable and inclusive society.

Economic Reforms and their Impact on Caste Disparities

In the Indian context, the caste system has long been recognized as a significant factor in perpetuating social inequality. The rigid hierarchical structure of the caste system has resulted in unequal access to resources, opportunities, and power for different caste groups.

However, the impact of economic reforms on caste disparities has been a subject of much debate and research among sociologists.

Economic reforms, initiated in the early 1990s, aimed to liberalize the Indian economy, promote privatization, and encourage foreign investment. These reforms brought about significant changes in the economic landscape of the country, leading to the growth of new industries, the expansion of the middle class, and increased urbanization. However, the question remains: did these reforms have any impact on caste-based inequalities?

Studies have shown that while economic reforms did contribute to overall economic growth, they did not necessarily lead to a reduction in caste disparities. In fact, in some cases, they may have even exacerbated existing inequalities. One reason for this is that the benefits of economic growth were not distributed equally among different caste groups. The upper castes, who already had access to resources and education, were better positioned to take advantage of the new opportunities created by economic reforms. As a result, they were able to consolidate their economic and social positions, widening the gap between them and the lower castes.

Another factor contributing to the persistence of caste disparities despite economic reforms is the social and cultural aspects associated with the caste system. The deeply ingrained notions of purity, pollution, and social hierarchy continue to influence social interactions, access to resources, and opportunities. Discrimination and exclusion based on caste identity still persist, hindering the upward mobility of lower caste individuals and communities.

Furthermore, economic reforms have also led to the emergence of new forms of inequality. The growth of the service and IT sectors, for instance, has created a demand for skilled workers, leading to a concentration of economic opportunities in urban areas. This has resulted in the migration of many individuals from rural areas, predominantly from lower caste backgrounds, in search of better economic prospects. However, their experiences in urban areas are often marked by exploitation, discrimination, and precarious working conditions.

In conclusion, economic reforms have not been able to address the deep-rooted caste disparities in Indian society. While they have contributed to overall economic growth, the benefits have not been evenly distributed, and existing inequalities have often been perpetuated or exacerbated. To truly address caste-based inequalities, it is essential to not only focus on economic reforms but also challenge the social, cultural, and political dimensions of the caste system. Only through a comprehensive and multi-dimensional approach can we hope to create a society that is truly equitable and just for all its citizens.

Chapter 6: Religious Justifications and Interpretations of the Indian Caste System

Caste in Hindu Scriptures and Mythology

The caste system has long been a deeply ingrained social structure in Indian society, with its roots traced back to ancient Hindu scriptures and mythology. This subchapter aims to explore the origins and religious justifications of the Indian caste system, shedding light on its historical evolution and impact on various aspects of society. Addressed to sociologists, this content delves into the intricate intersections between caste, education, social inequality, gender, and marginalized communities.

Hindu scriptures, such as the Manusmriti and the Puranas, provide religious justifications for the caste system. These texts describe the creation of the four varnas (castes) – Brahmins, Kshatriyas, Vaishyas, and Shudras – with each caste assigned specific duties and privileges based on their birth. The division of labor, as prescribed in these scriptures, is believed to maintain social order and harmony. However, it has also perpetuated social inequality by confining individuals to their caste-based professions and limiting their access to resources and opportunities.

One of the most significant impacts of the caste system is its effect on education. The subchapter discusses how caste-based discrimination has hindered access to education for lower-caste individuals, particularly Dalits (formerly known as untouchables) and other marginalized communities. It explores the barriers they face in pursuing education, including social exclusion, unequal resource allocation, and discriminatory practices within educational

PERPETUATING INEQUALITY: EXPLORING THE ROLE OF THE INDIAN CASTE SYSTEM

institutions. This analysis helps highlight the urgent need for reforms to address the educational disparities perpetuated by the caste system.

Furthermore, this subchapter examines the intersectionality of caste and gender, focusing on the experiences of women within the caste system. It explores how caste-based discrimination intersects with patriarchy, further marginalizing women and limiting their agency. The content also sheds light on the resistance movements led by Dalit women, who have challenged the intersectional oppression they face.

Additionally, this subchapter touches upon the economic consequences of the caste system, analyzing its impact on different social classes. It explores how caste-based discrimination affects economic opportunities, wealth distribution, and social mobility. This analysis helps to uncover the structural barriers that perpetuate economic inequality in Indian society.

Throughout the subchapter, the content emphasizes the need for understanding the historical origins and religious justifications of the caste system to effectively address and dismantle it. By exploring the impact of globalization and drawing international perspectives on caste discrimination, it also highlights the need for comparative studies and global solidarity against all forms of discrimination.

Overall, this subchapter provides sociologists with a comprehensive understanding of the role of caste in Hindu scriptures and mythology. It explores the intricate intersections between caste and various aspects of society, shedding light on the need for social, educational, and political reforms to dismantle the caste-based inequalities that persist in modern-day India.

Brahmanical Interpretations and Justifications

In the subchapter titled "Brahmanical Interpretations and Justifications," we delve into the religious justifications and interpretations that have perpetuated the Indian caste system. This exploration is crucial for sociologists seeking to understand the roots and mechanisms behind the deeply entrenched social inequality in India.

Religion plays a significant role in shaping societal structures, and the Indian caste system is no exception. Brahmanical interpretations of Hindu scriptures, such as the Vedas, Puranas, and Manusmriti, have been used to provide legitimacy and perpetuate the caste hierarchy. These interpretations have justified the division of society into four varnas, with Brahmins at the top, followed by Kshatriyas, Vaishyas, and Shudras.

According to these interpretations, each varna has specific duties and responsibilities, with Brahmins being the custodians of knowledge and spirituality. This belief in the inherent superiority of the Brahmins has been used to legitimize their dominance and maintain social order. They have been portrayed as the rightful leaders, while the lower castes are considered inferior by birth and destined to perform menial tasks.

Furthermore, Brahmanical interpretations have reinforced the notion of karma and reincarnation, suggesting that one's caste position is a result of their actions in past lives. This belief system implies that those born into lower castes are responsible for their own suffering and must accept their fate without question. It places the burden of social inequality on the oppressed rather than challenging the unjust system itself.

Sociologists studying the impact of the Indian caste system on access to education and its role in perpetuating social inequality will find this subchapter particularly relevant. By understanding the religious justifications and interpretations that sustain the caste system, scholars can develop a comprehensive understanding of how caste-based discrimination operates at both individual and systemic levels.

Additionally, examining Brahmanical interpretations through an intersectional lens is essential. Women and marginalized communities within each caste face multiple forms of discrimination and oppression. This subchapter will explore how gender, class, and caste intersect to shape the experiences of these individuals and further entrench social inequality.

By critically analyzing the historical origins and evolution of the Indian caste system, sociologists can gain insights into its economic consequences on different social classes. They can also examine how caste-based politics influence Indian elections and governance, as well as the resistance movements and empowerment efforts led by Dalits against the caste system.

Comparisons with other forms of discrimination and international perspectives on the Indian caste system will further enrich sociological research in this area, particularly in the context of globalization. Understanding the Brahmanical interpretations and justifications will contribute to a comprehensive and nuanced understanding of the Indian caste system and its impact on society.

Alternative Views and Criticisms from Within Hinduism

The Indian caste system has long been a subject of scrutiny and debate, and within the Hindu religion, there are various alternative views and criticisms that challenge its perpetuation and impact on society. This subchapter explores these perspectives, offering sociologists a deeper understanding of the complexities surrounding the Indian caste system.

One alternative view arises from within Hinduism itself, challenging the notion that the caste system is a fundamental aspect of the religion. Critics argue that the original Hindu scriptures, such as the Vedas and Upanishads, do not explicitly sanction the rigid caste hierarchy that exists today. Instead, they emphasize the importance of knowledge, virtue, and individual merit as determinants of one's social position. These alternative interpretations of Hindu texts highlight the potential for a more egalitarian society that transcends caste divisions.

Furthermore, sociologists examining the impact of the Indian caste system on access to education will find dissenting voices from within Hindu communities. Some progressive thinkers argue that education is the key to breaking the cycle of caste-based discrimination and social inequality. They advocate for equal educational opportunities for all, regardless of caste, and emphasize the need to challenge traditional notions of caste-based occupation and social mobility.

Another criticism from within Hinduism focuses on the experiences of women and marginalized communities. Intersectionality plays a crucial role in understanding how gender and caste intersect to create unique forms of discrimination. Activists and scholars argue that the caste system reinforces gender inequality and perpetuates the marginalization of women and other oppressed groups. By highlighting these voices, sociologists can gain insights into the lived experiences of those most affected by the caste system.

In addition to alternative views and criticisms, it is essential to explore the historical origins and evolution of the caste system to understand its complexities fully. By tracing its roots, sociologists can shed light on the social, economic, and political factors that contributed to its development and perpetuation over time.

Ultimately, this subchapter provides sociologists with a comprehensive understanding of the Indian caste system through alternative views and criticisms from within Hinduism. By examining these perspectives, sociologists can contribute to the ongoing discourse surrounding the impact of the caste system on education, social inequality, gender dynamics, and governance. This knowledge is crucial for developing

PERPETUATING INEQUALITY: EXPLORING THE ROLE OF THE INDIAN CASTE SYSTEM

effective strategies to address and challenge the caste system's detrimental effects and promote a more inclusive and equitable society.

Caste System in Other Religions in India

The Indian caste system is often associated with Hinduism, but it is essential to recognize that it has also permeated other religious communities in India. This subchapter aims to shed light on the presence and influence of the caste system in other religions in India, providing sociologists with a comprehensive understanding of its reach and impact.

One significant aspect to explore is the impact of the caste system on access to education. While the system has historically limited opportunities for those belonging to lower castes, this discrimination is not exclusive to Hinduism. By examining other religions, such as Islam, Christianity, Sikhism, and Buddhism, we can gain insights into how the caste system affects educational access across various religious communities.

Furthermore, understanding the role of the caste system in perpetuating social inequality is crucial. By studying the experiences of marginalized communities and women within different religious contexts, sociologists can analyze how the caste system intersects with other forms of discrimination and oppression. This intersectionality approach will contribute to a more comprehensive understanding of the challenges faced by these groups and the measures needed to address them effectively.

Exploring the historical origins and evolution of the caste system in other religions will also be insightful. By comparing these origins with the Hindu caste system, sociologists can identify commonalities and differences, which will aid in understanding the broader socio-cultural dynamics at play.

Additionally, it is essential to examine religious justifications and interpretations of the caste system. By delving into religious texts, rituals, and practices, sociologists can gain insights into how religious beliefs and traditions have contributed to the perpetuation and legitimation of the caste system within diverse religious communities.

The influence of the caste system in politics and governance, commonly referred to as caste-based politics, is another crucial area of study. Analyzing the role of caste in Indian elections and governance will provide sociologists with a nuanced understanding of how the caste system continues to shape power dynamics and social hierarchies in contemporary Indian society.

Furthermore, this subchapter should explore the resistance against the caste system and the empowerment movements led by Dalits. Examining these movements, their goals, and their challenges will help sociologists understand the strategies employed to challenge and dismantle the caste system, as well as the barriers they encounter.

Lastly, providing international perspectives on the Indian caste system and comparing it with other forms of discrimination will enhance sociologists' understanding of caste as a unique social phenomenon. By examining similarities and differences with other forms of discrimination globally, scholars can identify common patterns and unique aspects, contributing to a broader understanding of the caste system's complexity.

In conclusion, this subchapter aims to provide sociologists with a comprehensive understanding of the caste system in other religions in India. By exploring various aspects such as access to education, social inequality, intersectionality, historical origins, religious justifications, political influence, resistance movements, globalization's impact, and international comparisons, sociologists can develop a nuanced understanding of the caste system's reach and its implications for different religious communities in India.

Contemporary Challenges to Religious Justifications of Caste

In recent years, there has been a growing recognition of the inherent injustices and inequalities perpetuated by the Indian caste system. As sociologists, it is our duty to critically analyze and understand the various factors that contribute to the persistence of this system, including the religious justifications that have long been used to legitimize caste-based discrimination. This subchapter aims to shed light on the contemporary challenges faced by religious justifications of caste in India.

Traditionally, religious texts such as the Manusmriti have been cited as the basis for the hierarchical organization of society in India. However, many scholars and activists argue that these religious justifications are outdated and no longer hold relevance in the modern context. They contend that the caste system is a social construct, perpetuated by those in power to maintain their dominance and privilege.

One of the key challenges to religious justifications of caste lies in the increasing awareness and mobilization of marginalized communities, particularly Dalits, who have historically borne the brunt of caste-based discrimination. Dalit empowerment movements have gained significant momentum, challenging the notion that caste is divinely ordained and advocating for equal rights and opportunities for all individuals, regardless of their birth.

Moreover, the intersectional experiences of women and other marginalized communities within the caste system have further exposed the flaws in religious justifications. Women, in particular, have been subjected to multiple forms of discrimination due to their gender and caste. Their struggles and resistance have highlighted the need to critically examine and challenge religious interpretations that perpetuate their marginalization.

Furthermore, globalization has also played a role in challenging religious justifications of caste. Increased exposure to different cultures and ideas has led to a questioning of traditional beliefs and practices. As India becomes more interconnected with the global community, the legitimacy of the caste system and the religious justifications that support it are being called into question.

In conclusion, the contemporary challenges to religious justifications of caste underscore the need for a critical examination of the Indian caste system. As sociologists, we must continue to explore and document these challenges in order to contribute to the ongoing discourse on caste and social inequality. By doing so, we can work towards a more just and equitable society, where individuals are not defined by their birth but by their abilities and aspirations.

Chapter 7: Caste-based Politics: Analyzing the Influence of Caste in Indian Elections and Governance

Caste as a Determinant of Political Power

Introduction:

The Indian caste system has long been a significant determinant of social standing and access to resources in the country. This subchapter delves into the role of caste as a determinant of political power, exploring how caste influences political representation, election outcomes, and governance in India. By examining the intersectionality between caste and politics, sociologists can gain a deeper understanding of the complexities surrounding political power dynamics in the country.

Caste and Political Representation:

The impact of the Indian caste system on access to education and employment opportunities has resulted in unequal representation in political institutions. Historically, dominant castes have held the majority of political power, while marginalized communities, such as Dalits and tribal groups, have been underrepresented. This subchapter explores how caste-based politics perpetuates social inequality by limiting political representation for certain castes.

Caste and Election Outcomes:

The influence of caste in Indian elections is undeniable. Electoral strategies often revolve around appealing to specific caste groups, resulting in the fragmentation of the political landscape. Vote-bank politics, where political parties target specific caste groups for electoral gains, have further reinforced the role of caste in Indian politics. This subchapter analyzes the impact of caste on election outcomes and the subsequent governance decisions made by elected representatives.

Caste and Governance:

The influence of caste extends beyond electoral politics and permeates governance at various levels. Caste-based politics often leads to the allocation of resources and benefits based on caste affiliations, further perpetuating social inequality. The subchapter investigates how the Indian caste system shapes policy decisions, resource allocation, and the overall functioning of government institutions.

Conclusion:

Understanding the role of caste as a determinant of political power is crucial for sociologists studying the Indian caste system. By examining the intersectionality between caste and politics, one can comprehend the complex dynamics that perpetuate social inequality and hinder the realization of social justice. This subchapter provides valuable insights into the influence of caste on political representation, election outcomes, and governance in India. By shedding light on caste-based politics, it aims to contribute to the ongoing discourse on social justice and equality in the country.

Caste-Based Vote Banks and Electoral Strategies

In the diverse and complex landscape of Indian politics, caste-based vote banks have emerged as a prominent feature. This subchapter delves into the intricate connection between caste and electoral strategies, shedding light on the ways in which the Indian caste system influences voting patterns and shapes political outcomes.

Caste-based vote banks refer to groups of voters who align themselves with a particular caste or sub-caste, and politicians often target these groups to secure their support. Sociologists have long recognized the significance of caste as a determining factor in Indian elections, as it plays a crucial role in shaping political alliances and electoral strategies.

The impact of the Indian caste system on access to education has been widely studied, revealing a stark reality of inequality. Historically, certain castes have been systematically marginalized, resulting in limited educational opportunities. As a result, these marginalized groups often form their own vote banks, demanding political representation and policies that address their educational needs.

Moreover, the role of the Indian caste system in perpetuating social inequality cannot be overlooked. Caste-based vote banks often reinforce existing power structures, with dominant castes consolidating their political influence and marginalized communities struggling for equal representation. This subchapter explores the intricate dynamics of power and privilege that shape electoral strategies and decision-making processes.

Intersectionality and the Indian caste system are also examined in this subchapter, with a particular focus on the experiences of women and other marginalized communities. The intersectionality lens helps uncover the multiple layers of discrimination faced by individuals who belong to both lower castes and marginalized genders, highlighting the need for inclusive electoral strategies that address their unique challenges.

The historical origins and evolution of the Indian caste system are essential to understanding its continued influence in contemporary politics. By tracing the roots of this deeply entrenched social structure, sociologists can gain insights into how caste-based vote banks have evolved over time, adapting to changing political landscapes and societal dynamics.

Furthermore, the economic consequences of the Indian caste system on different social classes are explored. Caste-based vote banks often advocate for policies that address economic disparities and provide opportunities for upward mobility. Understanding the economic dimensions of caste-based electoral strategies is crucial for comprehending the broader societal implications.

Religious justifications and interpretations of the Indian caste system are also examined in this subchapter. Religion has played a significant role in perpetuating and justifying the caste system, and its influence on electoral strategies cannot be overlooked. By analyzing the religious dimensions, sociologists can gain insights into the deep-rooted beliefs and ideologies that shape electoral dynamics.

Caste-based politics and its influence on Indian elections and governance are thoroughly analyzed in this subchapter. The intricate web of caste-based alliances, identity politics, and electoral strategies are explored to provide a comprehensive understanding of the role of caste in shaping the political landscape.

Dalit empowerment movements and resistance against the Indian caste system are also examined. These movements have challenged the entrenched hierarchy and demanded equal representation and rights for marginalized communities. By studying the strategies and successes of these movements, sociologists can gain insights into the possibilities for social change and political transformation.

The impact of globalization on the Indian caste system is another crucial aspect discussed in this subchapter. Globalization has both challenged and reinforced caste-based identities, creating new dynamics and complexities in electoral strategies. By analyzing these global influences, sociologists can assess the extent to which globalization has transformed the caste system and its implications for electoral politics.

Lastly, international perspectives on the Indian caste system are explored, drawing comparisons with other forms of discrimination. By examining the similarities and differences between the Indian caste system and other systems of discrimination, sociologists can contribute to the broader discourse on social inequality and discrimination worldwide.

In conclusion, this subchapter provides a comprehensive exploration of caste-based vote banks and electoral strategies in the Indian context. By examining the intricate links between caste and politics, sociologists can gain a deeper understanding of the complexities of the Indian caste system and its wider implications for social inequality, representation, and political dynamics.

Reservation Policies and Political Representation

In the intricate web of social inequality perpetuated by the Indian caste system, the issue of reservation policies and political representation emerges as a crucial concern. This subchapter delves into the multifaceted dimensions of this issue, shedding light on the complex dynamics that shape the relationship between the caste system and political power in India.

Reservation policies, introduced as affirmative action measures, aim to redress historical injustices faced by marginalized communities. These policies seek to provide representation and opportunities to historically disadvantaged groups, such as Scheduled Castes, Scheduled Tribes, and Other Backward Classes, in various spheres of public life, including education and employment. Sociologists have extensively studied the impact of reservation policies on access to education, highlighting the transformative potential of such measures in dismantling caste-based barriers and empowering marginalized communities.

Moreover, this subchapter explores the role of the Indian caste system in perpetuating social inequality through the lens of political representation. By analyzing the influence of caste in Indian elections and governance, sociologists uncover how the caste system continues to shape power dynamics and hinder the realization of true democracy. The chapter investigates the complexities of caste-based politics, examining how caste affiliations influence voting patterns, candidate selection, and policy-making processes.

Intersectionality, a critical framework in sociological research, is applied to the Indian caste system to examine the experiences of women and marginalized communities. By unraveling the interplay between caste, gender, and other axes of social identity, scholars shed light on the unique challenges faced by Dalit women and other marginalized groups, who often bear the brunt of caste-based oppression and discrimination.

This subchapter also explores the historical origins and evolution of the Indian caste system, tracing its roots to ancient scriptures and societal stratification. By analyzing religious justifications and interpretations of the caste system, the chapter uncovers the intricate relationship between religion and social hierarchy. Furthermore, sociologists delve into the economic consequences of the caste system on different social classes, investigating how caste-based discrimination perpetuates economic disparities and hampers social mobility.

The subchapter concludes with an examination of Dalit empowerment movements and resistance against the Indian caste system. By highlighting the agency and resilience of marginalized communities, sociologists shed light on the transformative potential of grassroots movements in challenging caste-based oppression and advocating for social justice.

Overall, this subchapter offers a comprehensive analysis of reservation policies and political representation in the context of the Indian caste system. By addressing the concerns of sociologists and catering to the niches of the impact of the caste system on access to education, perpetuation of social inequality, intersectionality, historical origins, economic consequences, religious justifications, caste-based politics, Dalit empowerment movements, globalization's impact, and international perspectives, this chapter contributes to a deeper understanding of the complexities and implications of the Indian caste system in contemporary society.

Caste and Corruption in Politics

In this subchapter, we will delve into the intricate relationship between caste and corruption in Indian politics. As sociologists, it is crucial for us to understand how the caste system influences the political landscape and perpetuates social inequality in the country.

India's caste system is deeply entrenched in society and has significant ramifications for access to education, economic opportunities, and political power. The impact of the caste system on access to education is particularly noteworthy, as historically marginalized groups face formidable barriers and discrimination. This subchapter will explore how caste-based reservation policies and affirmative action measures have attempted to address this issue, but also how corruption in the education system perpetuates inequality.

Furthermore, we will analyze how the caste system reinforces social inequality through the lens of intersectionality. Women and marginalized communities often bear the brunt of caste-based discrimination, facing multiple layers of oppression. By examining their experiences, we can gain a more comprehensive understanding of the far-reaching consequences of the caste system on various social groups.

To comprehend the present-day implications of caste-based politics, we need to explore its historical origins and evolution. This subchapter will provide an overview of how the caste system transformed from a social hierarchy to a political tool, influencing elections and governance. We will examine how political parties strategically exploit caste identities to gain electoral advantage and perpetuate a system of patronage and corruption.

Dalit empowerment movements and resistance against the caste system will also be explored, as they play a crucial role in challenging the status quo and advocating for social justice. This subchapter will highlight the efforts of various social activists and organizations in fighting against caste-based discrimination and corruption in politics.

In the context of globalization, we will investigate how the Indian caste system is affected by international influences and interactions. This will involve an analysis of how globalization has both challenged and reinforced caste-based inequalities, as well as the implications for India's position in the global economy.

Lastly, we will widen our perspective and compare the Indian caste system with other forms of discrimination and social hierarchies around the world. By examining international perspectives, we can gain valuable insights into the similarities and differences between different systems of inequality.

Overall, this subchapter aims to provide sociologists with a comprehensive understanding of the interplay between caste, corruption, and politics in India. By delving into these complex issues, we can contribute to the ongoing discourse on social inequality and work towards a more equitable society for all.

Challenges and Prospects for Caste-based Political Mobilization

PERPETUATING INEQUALITY: EXPLORING THE ROLE OF THE INDIAN CASTE SYSTEM

The Indian caste system has played a significant role in shaping the political landscape of the country. Caste-based political mobilization refers to the process in which caste communities organize themselves to assert their political rights and secure representation in the government. This subchapter explores the challenges and prospects associated with caste-based political mobilization in India.

One of the major challenges faced by caste-based political mobilization is the diverse nature of the Indian caste system itself. With thousands of castes and sub-castes, each with its own distinctive identity and interests, mobilizing them under a single political banner can be a daunting task. Furthermore, the hierarchical nature of the caste system often leads to internal divisions and conflicts within caste communities, making it challenging to present a united front in the political arena.

Another challenge is the intersectionality of caste with other forms of discrimination, such as gender and socio-economic status. Women and marginalized communities within caste groups often face multiple layers of oppression and exclusion. Addressing their specific concerns and ensuring their active participation in political mobilization is crucial for creating an inclusive and representative political system.

Despite these challenges, caste-based political mobilization holds significant prospects for addressing social inequality and promoting the interests of marginalized communities. It provides a platform for historically disadvantaged groups to voice their grievances and demand social justice. By mobilizing caste communities, political parties can bring the concerns of the marginalized to the forefront of the political agenda, leading to policy interventions that aim to reduce caste-based discrimination and inequality.

Caste-based political mobilization also has the potential to challenge the dominant narrative of religious justifications and interpretations of the caste system. By emphasizing social and economic issues, political mobilization can shift the discourse from religious identity to issues of social justice and equal opportunities for all.

Furthermore, the impact of globalization on the Indian caste system has opened up new avenues for political mobilization. Global networks and transnational activism have facilitated the exchange of ideas and strategies for challenging the caste system. International perspectives on discrimination and inequality have provided valuable insights and comparisons, enabling activists and sociologists to develop effective strategies to combat caste-based discrimination.

In conclusion, caste-based political mobilization faces numerous challenges due to the diverse and hierarchical nature of the Indian caste system. However, it also offers significant prospects for addressing social inequality, empowering marginalized communities, and challenging the religious justifications of the caste system. By examining the challenges and prospects of caste-based political mobilization, sociologists can contribute to a deeper understanding of the role of the caste system in Indian politics and society.

Chapter 8: Dalit Empowerment Movements and Resistance Against the Indian Caste System

Formation and History of Dalit Movements

The formation and history of Dalit movements in India have played a significant role in challenging and resisting the oppressive Indian caste system. Dalits, also known as "untouchables," have historically been marginalized and oppressed by the higher castes, facing discrimination and exclusion in various aspects of their lives. This subchapter aims to explore the emergence, evolution, and impact of Dalit movements on Indian society, particularly focusing on the social, political, and economic aspects of their struggle.

Dalit movements trace their roots back to the late 19th century, with the emergence of leaders like Jyotirao Phule and Babasaheb Ambedkar. These leaders were instrumental in mobilizing Dalits, advocating for their rights, and challenging the caste-based social hierarchy. They recognized the need for collective action to address the deep-rooted inequalities perpetuated by the caste system.

The Dalit movement gained momentum during the Indian independence struggle, as Dalit leaders actively participated in the fight against British colonial rule. These leaders, inspired by the principles of equality and justice, demanded not only political freedom but also social liberation from the shackles of caste discrimination.

One of the major milestones in the Dalit movement was the formation of the Dalit Panther movement in the 1970s. This movement aimed to unite Dalits across different regions and castes, emphasizing self-respect, self-assertion, and self-determination. It challenged the dominant narrative of caste-based superiority and redefined Dalit identity based on pride and resilience.

Over the years, Dalit movements have been successful in securing legal protections and affirmative action policies through the Indian Constitution. The reservation system, for instance, provides reserved seats for Dalits in education, employment, and politics, aiming to address historical injustices and promote social inclusion.

However, despite these advancements, Dalits continue to face discrimination and violence in various forms. The subchapter will also shed light on the ongoing challenges faced by Dalit communities, including limited access to education, economic opportunities, and political representation.

By examining the formation and history of Dalit movements, this subchapter aims to provide sociologists with a comprehensive understanding of the struggles faced by marginalized communities in India. It highlights the intersectionality of caste, gender, and class, and the need for holistic approaches to tackle social inequality. Additionally, it invites sociologists to consider international perspectives and draw comparisons with other forms of discrimination, contributing to a global discourse on social justice and equality.

Dalit Literature and Art as Tools of Resistance

Dalit Literature and Art as Tools of Resistance is a subchapter that sheds light on the powerful role that literature and art play in challenging and dismantling the Indian caste system. This section aims to explore the ways in which Dalit writers and artists have used their creative expression to voice their experiences, challenge social norms, and inspire social change.

Dalit literature and art have emerged as significant tools of resistance against the Indian caste system. Dalit writers and artists have found solace and strength in their creative endeavors, using them as platforms to expose the deep-rooted inequalities perpetuated by the caste system. Through their work, they provide a unique perspective on the experiences of Dalit individuals and communities, highlighting their struggles, aspirations, and resilience.

Dalit literature encompasses a wide range of written works, including autobiographies, novels, poetry, and plays. These literary pieces delve into the everyday realities faced by Dalits, addressing issues such as discrimination, untouchability, social exclusion, and violence. By sharing their stories, Dalit writers challenge mainstream narratives, disrupt dominant discourses, and humanize their experiences. Their writings serve as a powerful form of resistance, aiming to create awareness, empathy, and social transformation.

Similarly, Dalit art has emerged as a potent tool of resistance. Through various art forms such as painting, sculpture, photography, and performance, Dalit artists express their lived experiences and challenge the caste-based hierarchy. Their artworks often confront the viewer with the stark realities of caste-based discrimination, forcing them to confront their own biases and engage in dialogue about social justice.

Dalit literature and art also provide a sense of empowerment and identity to Dalit communities. By celebrating their culture, heritage, and history, Dalit writers and artists reclaim their narrative and challenge the dominant caste-based narratives that have marginalized and silenced them for centuries. In doing so, they inspire other marginalized communities to resist and challenge the caste system, fostering solidarity and unity among oppressed groups.

The subchapter "Dalit Literature and Art as Tools of Resistance" aims to highlight the profound impact that creative expression has on challenging and dismantling the Indian caste system. By analyzing the works of Dalit writers and artists, sociologists can gain a deeper understanding of the experiences of marginalized communities, the power of art as a tool for social change, and the potential pathways to creating a more equal and just society.

Dalit Activism and Struggles for Social Justice

Dalit activism is at the forefront of the fight against the Indian caste system, driven by the pursuit of social justice and equality. Sociologists studying the impact of the Indian caste system on access to education recognize the significant barriers faced by Dalits in their pursuit of education. Dalits, historically marginalized and oppressed, have been systematically denied educational opportunities, perpetuating social inequality. This subchapter delves into the struggles faced by Dalits in their quest for education and the activism that has emerged as a result.

Intersectionality plays a crucial role in understanding the experiences of Dalit women and other marginalized communities within the Indian caste system. Examining the unique challenges faced by Dalit women sheds light on the multiple layers of discrimination they face, compounding the effects of caste-based oppression. Sociologists investigating this intersectionality aim to highlight the urgent need for inclusive policies and social reform.

The historical origins and evolution of the Indian caste system provide context for understanding its deep-rooted impact on social inequality. By tracing its development through the centuries, sociologists gain insights into the structural mechanisms that perpetuate caste-based discrimination and the ways in which it has morphed over time.

Economically, the Indian caste system has far-reaching consequences on different social classes. The subchapter explores the disparities in wealth, employment opportunities, and social mobility faced by Dalits and other caste groups. It also examines the role of the caste system in maintaining economic inequality and hindering upward mobility for marginalized communities.

Religious justifications and interpretations of the caste system are explored, shedding light on how religious texts have been manipulated to legitimize and perpetuate caste-based discrimination. Sociologists critically analyze these justifications to challenge the religious and moral foundations of the caste system.

Caste-based politics in Indian elections and governance is a key aspect that sociologists delve into, analyzing the influence of caste dynamics on political power structures. This subchapter examines the role of caste in shaping political identities and influencing electoral outcomes, shedding light on the interplay between caste and politics.

Dalit empowerment movements and resistance against the caste system are explored, highlighting the struggles and achievements of Dalit activists. Sociologists analyze the strategies employed by these movements and the impact they have had on challenging social norms and fighting for social justice.

The impact of globalization on the Indian caste system is examined, with sociologists investigating how globalization has both challenged and reinforced caste-based discrimination. The subchapter explores the implications of globalization on caste-based identities, economic opportunities, and social mobility.

International perspectives on the Indian caste system are also included, drawing comparisons with other forms of discrimination around the world. Sociologists examine the similarities and differences between the Indian caste system and other systems of oppression, further illuminating the global significance of the struggles for social justice in India.

In conclusion, this subchapter provides sociologists with a comprehensive understanding of Dalit activism and the efforts to combat the Indian caste system. By examining various aspects such as education, intersectionality, historical origins, economic consequences, religious justifications, politics, globalization, and international perspectives, researchers gain insights into the complexities of caste-based discrimination and the ongoing fight for social equality in India.

Legal and Constitutional Interventions for Dalit Rights

The Indian caste system has long been a source of social inequality and injustice, particularly for Dalits, who are at the bottom of the caste hierarchy. However, over the years, there have been significant legal and constitutional interventions aimed at addressing and rectifying the discrimination and marginalization faced by Dalits in India. This subchapter will delve into the various legal and constitutional measures that have been implemented to safeguard Dalit rights.

One of the most important legal interventions for Dalit rights is the reservation system. Affirmative action policies, enshrined in the Indian Constitution, ensure that a certain percentage of government jobs, educational institutions, and political positions are reserved for Dalits. This reservation system has been instrumental in providing opportunities and access to education and employment that were previously denied to Dalits due to their caste.

The Scheduled Castes and Scheduled Tribes (Prevention of Atrocities) Act is another crucial legislative measure that seeks to protect Dalits from caste-based violence and discrimination. This act not only criminalizes offenses committed against Dalits but also establishes special courts for the speedy resolution of cases related to atrocities against them. It has played a vital role in creating a deterrent effect and ensuring justice for Dalits.

Additionally, the constitutional provision of the Right to Equality guarantees equal protection under the law and prohibits discrimination based on caste. This has been instrumental in challenging discriminatory practices and promoting a more inclusive society.

Moreover, the judiciary has played a pivotal role in interpreting and enforcing laws related to Dalit rights. Landmark judgments such as the Indra Sawhney case, commonly known as the Mandal Commission case, upheld the reservation system and reaffirmed the importance of affirmative action in addressing historical injustices.

However, despite these legal and constitutional interventions, challenges persist in fully realizing Dalit rights. Implementation gaps, systemic biases, and societal attitudes continue to hinder the effective enforcement of these measures. Therefore, it is essential for sociologists and researchers to critically examine the impact and effectiveness of these legal interventions and advocate for further reforms to ensure the eradication of caste-based discrimination and the empowerment of Dalits.

By analyzing the legal and constitutional interventions for Dalit rights, sociologists can gain a comprehensive understanding of the progress made and the areas that require further attention. This knowledge can contribute to ongoing efforts to dismantle the Indian caste system and promote social equality and justice for all marginalized communities in India.

International Solidarity and Support for Dalit Empowerment

The Indian caste system has long been a subject of interest for sociologists, as it plays a significant role in perpetuating social inequality and limiting access to education for certain groups. One such marginalized community that has borne the brunt of the caste system is the Dalit community. This subchapter will delve into the importance of international solidarity and support for Dalit empowerment.

The impact of the Indian caste system on access to education is deeply concerning. Dalits, historically referred to as "untouchables," have been systematically excluded from educational opportunities. This has resulted in a cycle of poverty and limited social mobility within the community. Sociologists have extensively studied how the caste system perpetuates social inequality and restricts upward mobility, making it imperative to address these issues through international solidarity.

The experiences of Dalit women and other marginalized communities within the Indian caste system deserve special attention. Intersectionality, the overlapping of various forms of discrimination, further exacerbates their marginalization. International support can help shed light on the unique struggles faced by Dalit women and promote their empowerment, leading to a more inclusive society.

Understanding the historical origins and evolution of the Indian caste system is crucial in comprehending its impact on contemporary society. By examining the economic consequences of the caste system on different social classes, sociologists can better grasp the structural inequalities that hinder social progress. International solidarity can aid in fostering a global understanding of the caste system and encourage collective efforts to dismantle it.

Religious justifications and interpretations have played a significant role in perpetuating the caste system. By critically analyzing these religious beliefs and challenging their discriminatory aspects, sociologists can contribute to the dismantling of caste-based discrimination. International perspectives on the Indian caste system, drawing comparisons with other forms of discrimination, can provide valuable insights and strategies for combating caste-based oppression.

Dalit empowerment movements have emerged as a powerful force against the Indian caste system. International solidarity and support can amplify their efforts and provide a platform for their voices to be heard. By highlighting the resistance against the caste system, this subchapter aims to inspire sociologists to engage with and support these movements.

Lastly, the impact of globalization on the Indian caste system cannot be ignored. As India becomes increasingly interconnected with the global economy, the caste system faces new challenges and opportunities. Sociologists must explore these dynamics and their implications for Dalit empowerment.

In conclusion, international solidarity and support are essential in the journey towards Dalit empowerment and dismantling the Indian caste system. By engaging with the issues raised in this subchapter, sociologists can contribute to a more inclusive and equal society. It is imperative that we stand in solidarity with the marginalized communities affected by the caste system and work towards their empowerment on a global scale.

Chapter 9: The Impact of Globalization on the Indian Caste System

Globalization and Economic Liberalization

Globalization and economic liberalization have had a profound impact on the Indian caste system, both in terms of exacerbating existing inequalities and opening up new opportunities for social mobility. This subchapter seeks to explore and analyze the complex relationship between globalization, economic liberalization, and the perpetuation of the Indian caste system.

One of the key consequences of globalization and economic liberalization is the impact on access to education. Historically, the Indian caste system has limited educational opportunities for lower castes, leading to a perpetuation of social inequality. However, with the advent of globalization and economic liberalization, there has been an increase in private educational institutions and foreign universities in India. This has created new avenues for education and a potential for social mobility for marginalized communities. Sociologists must critically examine the extent to which globalization has truly improved access to education for lower castes, and whether it has led to a reduction in social inequality.

Furthermore, globalization has also brought to light the intersectionality of the Indian caste system, particularly in relation to women and marginalized communities. Women from lower castes often face multiple forms of discrimination, and globalization has both amplified these challenges and provided opportunities for resistance and empowerment. Sociologists must delve into the experiences of women and marginalized communities, examining how globalization both perpetuates their marginalization and provides them with platforms for activism and change.

PERPETUATING INEQUALITY: EXPLORING THE ROLE OF THE INDIAN CASTE SYSTEM

The historical origins and evolution of the Indian caste system cannot be ignored when discussing its relationship with globalization and economic liberalization. Understanding the caste system's roots is crucial in comprehending its continued influence in contemporary Indian society. Additionally, sociologists must examine the economic consequences of the caste system on different social classes. Globalization and economic liberalization have led to economic disparities and income inequality, with certain castes benefiting more than others. An analysis of these disparities is crucial to understanding the impact of globalization on the Indian caste system.

Religious justifications and interpretations of the caste system also play a significant role in perpetuating its existence. Sociologists must delve into the religious ideologies that have historically supported the caste system and explore how these ideologies have been affected by globalization. Similarly, the influence of caste on politics and governance in India cannot be overlooked. Caste-based politics shape electoral strategies and policy decisions, and an examination of these dynamics is essential.

Finally, sociologists must explore the resistance and empowerment movements that have emerged in response to the caste system. Dalit empowerment movements have gained momentum in recent years, challenging the caste hierarchy and advocating for social justice. These movements are often influenced by global human rights discourses and have the potential to bring about significant change.

Overall, this subchapter aims to provide sociologists with a nuanced understanding of the relationship between globalization, economic liberalization, and the perpetuation of the Indian caste system. By examining various dimensions of the caste system within the context of globalization, sociologists can contribute to the ongoing discourse on social inequality and advocate for a more equitable society.

Caste and Global Labor Market Dynamics

The Indian caste system has had a profound impact on various aspects of society, including the global labor market dynamics. This subchapter explores how the caste system influences access to employment opportunities, perpetuates social inequality, and affects marginalized communities and women. It also delves into the historical origins of the caste system, its economic consequences on different social classes, religious justifications, and interpretations.

The Indian caste system has played a significant role in shaping access to education and employment. The hierarchical nature of the caste system has led to unequal opportunities for individuals from lower castes, limiting their access to quality education and thus hindering their chances to compete in the global labor market. This perpetuates social inequality and reinforces the dominance of higher castes in professional and managerial positions.

Moreover, the intersectionality of caste and gender exacerbates the discrimination faced by women from marginalized communities. They face multiple layers of discrimination, making it even more challenging for them to access employment opportunities and break free from the cycle of poverty and social exclusion.

To understand the impact of the caste system, it is essential to examine its historical origins and evolution. The caste system emerged thousands of years ago and has since evolved, adapting to changing social and economic dynamics. Understanding its historical context helps in comprehending its persistence and resistance against efforts to eradicate it.

Economically, the caste system has profound consequences on different social classes. It creates a system where certain castes have access to better economic opportunities, while others are confined to menial and low-paying jobs. This perpetuates social stratification and hinders social mobility, contributing to the disparities in wealth and income distribution.

Religious justifications and interpretations of the caste system also play a crucial role in its perpetuation. The subchapter delves into the various religious beliefs and practices that have been used to legitimize and reinforce the caste hierarchy. By exploring these religious aspects, sociologists can gain a comprehensive understanding of the caste system's entrenched nature.

Furthermore, this subchapter addresses the influence of the caste system on Indian politics and governance. Caste-based politics are prevalent in India, with caste affiliation often determining electoral outcomes. Analyzing the role of caste in politics helps shed light on the systemic biases and challenges faced by marginalized communities in a democratic framework.

The subchapter also explores the resistance and empowerment movements by Dalits, who are historically considered the lowest caste. These movements aim to challenge and dismantle the caste system, advocating for social justice and equality. Studying these movements provides insights into the transformative power of collective action and the potential for change.

Globalization has had both positive and negative impacts on the Indian caste system. On one hand, globalization has exposed caste-based inequalities to international scrutiny, leading to increased awareness and advocacy for change. On the other hand, globalization has contributed to the commodification of labor, leading to the exploitation of marginalized communities and perpetuating their disadvantaged position in the global labor market.

Lastly, the subchapter examines international perspectives on the Indian caste system, drawing comparisons with other forms of discrimination. By analyzing similarities and differences, sociologists can gain a broader understanding of how caste-based discrimination compares to other forms of social inequality and discrimination worldwide.

In conclusion, this subchapter explores the multifaceted role of the Indian caste system in shaping global labor market dynamics. It highlights the impact of the caste system on access to education, perpetuation of social inequality, experiences of women and marginalized communities, historical origins, economic consequences, religious justifications, caste-based politics, resistance movements, globalization, and international perspectives. By comprehensively examining these aspects, sociologists can gain valuable insights into the complexities and challenges posed by the Indian caste system in contemporary society.

Transnational Movements and Diaspora Communities

In the subchapter titled "Transnational Movements and Diaspora Communities," we delve into the far-reaching impacts of the Indian caste system on individuals and communities across the globe. As sociologists, it is crucial for us to understand how the caste system extends beyond the borders of India and influences the lives of diaspora communities.

The Indian caste system has had a significant impact on access to education, perpetuating social inequality in both India and diaspora communities. We explore how the rigidity of the caste system limits educational opportunities for lower caste individuals, hindering their upward mobility and reinforcing social stratification. Through case studies and empirical evidence, we uncover the barriers faced by marginalized communities, particularly women, in acquiring quality education.

Intersectionality plays a crucial role in understanding the experiences of women and marginalized communities within the Indian caste system. By examining the intersections of caste, gender, and other social identities, we shed light on the unique challenges faced by these individuals. We explore the ways in which discrimination based on caste intersects with gender inequality, exacerbating the marginalization of women from lower castes.

To truly comprehend the Indian caste system, we must delve into its historical origins and evolution. By tracing its roots and understanding its development over time, we gain insight into the deep-seated nature of caste-based discrimination. We explore how historical factors, such as colonization, have shaped and perpetuated the caste system, leading to its continued existence today.

The economic consequences of the Indian caste system on different social classes are also explored in this subchapter. We analyze how caste-based discrimination hinders economic mobility and perpetuates socioeconomic disparities. By examining the linkages between caste and economic opportunities, we gain a comprehensive understanding of the structural inequalities that persist within Indian society and diaspora communities.

Religious justifications and interpretations of the Indian caste system are another important aspect to consider. We delve into the religious texts and ideologies that have been used to justify and maintain the caste system. By critically analyzing these interpretations, we challenge the religious foundations that perpetuate discrimination and social exclusion.

Caste-based politics and its influence on Indian elections and governance are also examined in this subchapter. We analyze the role of caste in shaping political power dynamics and policy-making processes. By understanding the influence of caste in the political arena, we gain insights into the challenges of building an inclusive and equitable society.

Furthermore, we explore the Dalit empowerment movements and resistance against the Indian caste system. By highlighting the voices and experiences of Dalit activists, we shed light on the struggles and successes of those fighting against caste-based discrimination. We examine the strategies employed by these movements and their impact on challenging the entrenched caste hierarchy.

Globalization has had a profound impact on the Indian caste system, and we explore its consequences in this subchapter. We analyze how globalization has both reinforced and challenged caste-based discrimination. By examining the ways in which globalization intersects with the caste system, we gain a broader perspective on the complexities of social change in the modern world.

Finally, we provide international perspectives on the Indian caste system by comparing it to other forms of discrimination. By drawing parallels and analyzing similarities, we enhance our understanding of the universality of discrimination and the unique aspects of the Indian caste system.

In conclusion, "Transnational Movements and Diaspora Communities" delves into the various dimensions and consequences of the Indian caste system beyond the borders of India. By examining its impact on education, social inequality, intersectionality, historical origins, economic consequences, religious justifications, politics, resistance movements, globalization, and international perspectives, we strive to provide a comprehensive understanding of the far-reaching implications of the Indian caste system.

Global Advocacy against Caste Discrimination

Caste discrimination in India has persisted for centuries, perpetuating social inequality and hindering access to education and opportunities for marginalized communities. As sociologists, it is crucial for us to understand and address the impact of the Indian caste system, not only within the country but also on a global scale. This subchapter explores the efforts made by various global advocacy groups to combat caste discrimination and promote equality.

The Indian caste system has long been a subject of scrutiny and concern for sociologists worldwide. Recognizing the significance of addressing this issue, international organizations and human rights groups have joined forces to advocate against caste discrimination. These movements aim to raise awareness, challenge discriminatory practices, and foster inclusive societies.

One of the primary concerns regarding the Indian caste system is its impact on access to education. Dalits, also known as the "untouchables," face severe discrimination in educational institutions, limiting their chances for social mobility. Global advocacy groups have been instrumental in highlighting these inequalities and pressuring governments to implement policies that ensure equal educational opportunities for all.

Moreover, the role of the Indian caste system in perpetuating social inequality cannot be overlooked. Marginalized communities, particularly women, face intersecting forms of discrimination due to their caste and gender. Global advocacy efforts have shed light on the experiences of these communities, emphasizing the need for intersectional approaches to address caste discrimination.

Understanding the historical origins and evolution of the caste system is crucial in comprehending its present-day implications. Advocacy groups have worked towards documenting and analyzing the caste system's historical context, seeking to challenge religious justifications and interpretations that perpetuate discrimination.

Caste-based politics and its influence on Indian elections and governance have also been subjects of study. Global advocacy efforts have helped in analyzing the role of caste in politics, identifying its impact on decision-making processes and policies. By highlighting these issues, advocacy groups aim to promote political inclusion and representation for marginalized communities.

Dalit empowerment movements have emerged as vital sources of resistance against the caste system. Global advocacy has played a crucial role in supporting these movements, amplifying their voices, and fostering solidarity across borders. These efforts have helped bring international attention to the struggles faced by Dalits and other marginalized communities in India.

Furthermore, globalization has both positive and negative consequences on the Indian caste system. Advocacy groups have explored the ways in which globalization has influenced caste dynamics, examining its impact on labor migration, economic disparities, and social hierarchies. These insights are crucial in understanding the complexities of caste discrimination in a globalized world.

Lastly, international perspectives on the Indian caste system have been essential in drawing comparisons with other forms of discrimination. By examining similarities and differences, global advocacy groups aim to learn from other anti-discrimination movements and develop effective strategies to combat caste-based discrimination.

In conclusion, global advocacy against caste discrimination has played a significant role in addressing the impacts of the Indian caste system. By focusing on issues such as access to education, social inequality, intersectionality, historical origins, economic consequences, religious justifications, caste-based politics, Dalit empowerment, globalization, and international perspectives, these efforts have shed light on the need for a more inclusive and equal society. As sociologists, it is crucial for us to recognize the importance of these advocacy movements and continue to support their endeavors to eradicate caste discrimination.

Challenges and Opportunities for Caste Equality in a Globalized World

In recent years, the Indian caste system has come under scrutiny for its role in perpetuating social inequality and hindering access to education. As sociologists, it is crucial to understand the challenges and opportunities for caste equality in a globalized world. This subchapter aims to shed light on the various dimensions of this issue, exploring its impact on education, social inequality, intersectionality, historical origins, economic consequences, religious justifications, politics, resistance movements, globalization, and international perspectives.

The impact of the Indian caste system on access to education is a pressing concern. Dalits and other marginalized communities continue to face discrimination and exclusion, depriving them of educational opportunities. This perpetuates social inequality and reinforces caste-based divisions. Sociologists must analyze the structural barriers that hinder educational access and advocate for policies that promote equal opportunities for all.

Intersectionality plays a significant role in the experiences of women and marginalized communities within the caste system. Women face multiple forms of discrimination due to their gender and caste.

Understanding their unique challenges and experiences is vital for devising comprehensive strategies to address caste-based inequality.

Exploring the historical origins and evolution of the Indian caste system helps sociologists trace its roots and understand its persistence in contemporary society. This historical context provides insights into the deeply entrenched social structures that perpetuate inequality.

The economic consequences of the caste system on different social classes are significant. While the upper castes often enjoy economic benefits, Dalits and lower castes face economic marginalization. Analyzing these disparities allows sociologists to propose policies that promote economic equality and social mobility.

Religious justifications and interpretations of the caste system also contribute to its perpetuation. Sociologists must critically examine these beliefs, challenging any religiously sanctioned discrimination and promoting inclusive interpretations of religious texts.

Caste-based politics and its influence on Indian elections and governance are critical areas of study. Understanding the role of caste in politics helps us comprehend its impact on social policies and democratic processes.

Dalit empowerment movements and resistance against the caste system are noteworthy developments in recent years. Sociologists should explore the strategies employed by these movements, assess their effectiveness, and support their efforts to eradicate caste-based discrimination.

The impact of globalization on the Indian caste system is an emerging area of research. Globalization has both positive and negative consequences for caste equality, and sociologists must examine these dynamics to identify opportunities for progress.

Finally, international perspectives on the Indian caste system provide valuable insights by comparing it with other forms of discrimination worldwide. Exploring these connections helps us understand the global nature of inequality and find common ground in the fight against discrimination.

In conclusion, this subchapter addresses the challenges and opportunities for caste equality in a globalized world. By examining various aspects of the Indian caste system, sociologists can contribute to the ongoing discourse and work towards a more equitable society.

Chapter 10: International Perspectives on the Indian Caste System: Comparisons with Other Forms of Discrimination

Caste Discrimination in a Global Context

Caste discrimination is a deeply rooted social issue that has persisted for centuries in India. However, its impact extends beyond the borders of the country, making it a global concern. This subchapter aims to explore the manifestations and consequences of caste discrimination in a broader context, shedding light on its significance for sociologists and various niches interested in the Indian caste system.

One crucial area where caste discrimination has a profound impact is access to education. The Indian caste system has historically restricted educational opportunities for lower castes, perpetuating social inequality. Sociologists studying the impact of the caste system on education will find valuable insights into the barriers faced by marginalized communities and the implications for their social mobility and overall well-being.

Examining the role of the Indian caste system in perpetuating social inequality is another area of concern. The hierarchical nature of the caste system perpetuates discrimination and marginalization, leading to unequal distribution of resources and opportunities. Sociologists exploring this topic will gain a deeper understanding of how the caste system continues to shape social relationships and power structures in Indian society.

Intersectionality is a critical lens through which to examine the experiences of women and marginalized communities within the

Indian caste system. Sociologists delving into this niche will explore how caste discrimination intersects with gender, class, and other social identities, resulting in unique forms of oppression and exclusion.

Understanding the historical origins and evolution of the Indian caste system is essential to grasp its complexities fully. By tracing its roots and development over time, sociologists can analyze the structural and cultural factors that have contributed to its persistence and resilience.

Economists and sociologists interested in the economic consequences of the caste system will find a rich field of study. The caste system has significant implications for different social classes, affecting their access to resources, job opportunities, and economic mobility.

Religious justifications and interpretations of the Indian caste system also merit exploration. Sociologists examining this aspect will analyze how religious beliefs and practices have both reinforced and challenged the caste system, shaping societal attitudes and behaviors.

Caste-based politics is another crucial area of study. By analyzing the influence of caste in Indian elections and governance, sociologists can unravel the intricate relationship between caste, power, and political representation.

Dalit empowerment movements and resistance against the caste system offer valuable insights into the potential for social change and transformation. Sociologists examining these movements will gain a deeper understanding of the challenges faced by marginalized communities and the strategies employed to challenge caste discrimination.

Globalization has had a profound impact on the Indian caste system. Sociologists exploring this topic will explore how globalization has both exacerbated and challenged caste discrimination, creating new dynamics and opportunities for social change.

Finally, international perspectives on the Indian caste system provide a comparative lens to understand caste discrimination in relation to other forms of discrimination worldwide. Sociologists interested in the broader study of discrimination and social inequality will find valuable insights for their research and analysis.

In conclusion, this subchapter on caste discrimination in a global context offers a comprehensive exploration of the Indian caste system's impact on various aspects of society. It provides a rich ground for sociologists and other specialists interested in understanding and addressing the complexities and consequences of caste discrimination.

Comparisons with Racism and Apartheid

In exploring the role of the Indian caste system, it is imperative to draw comparisons with other forms of discrimination, such as racism and apartheid. By examining these parallels, we can gain a deeper understanding of the complexities and consequences of the caste system and its impact on various aspects of society.

Racism, much like the Indian caste system, is a system of social stratification that categorizes individuals based on their perceived racial or ethnic backgrounds. Both racism and casteism perpetuate social inequality by creating hierarchies and limiting opportunities for marginalized communities.

Apartheid, the system of racial segregation enforced in South Africa, shares similarities with the Indian caste system in terms of institutionalized discrimination and the denial of basic rights. Both systems enforce social boundaries and restrict access to resources and opportunities based on one's birth status.

The impact of the Indian caste system on access to education is comparable to the effects of racism and apartheid on educational opportunities for marginalized groups. Dalits and other lower caste individuals often face barriers in accessing quality education, limiting their social mobility and perpetuating inequality.

Intersectionality, a concept that examines how different forms of discrimination intersect and compound each other, is crucial in understanding the experiences of women and marginalized communities within the Indian caste system. Women from lower castes face dual forms of discrimination based on their gender and caste, which further exacerbates their marginalization.

The historical origins and evolution of the Indian caste system can be analyzed in relation to the historical context of racism and apartheid. Understanding the roots of these systems helps us comprehend the complexities and long-lasting effects they have had on society.

The economic consequences of the Indian caste system, similar to apartheid, have resulted in significant disparities between different social classes. Higher caste individuals often have greater access to resources, wealth, and opportunities, while lower caste individuals are trapped in cycles of poverty and exploitation.

Religious justifications and interpretations of the Indian caste system can be compared to the ways in which religion has been used to justify racism and apartheid. These religious justifications have perpetuated a system of discrimination and oppression.

Analyzing the influence of caste in Indian politics and governance is comparable to examining the role of race in political systems affected by racism and apartheid. Caste-based politics have a significant impact on elections and policymaking, further entrenching caste-based discrimination.

Dalit empowerment movements and resistance against the Indian caste system can be seen as analogous to the anti-apartheid and civil rights movements. These movements strive to challenge and dismantle the oppressive structures that perpetuate inequality.

Lastly, international perspectives on the Indian caste system provide valuable insights by drawing comparisons with other forms of discrimination worldwide. By understanding the commonalities and differences between these systems, we can foster a global dialogue on combating discrimination and promoting equality.

In conclusion, comparing the Indian caste system with racism and apartheid sheds light on the far-reaching consequences of this social hierarchy. By examining these comparisons, we can better comprehend the role of the caste system in perpetuating social inequality, limiting access to education, and marginalizing women and marginalized communities. Understanding these parallels is vital for sociologists and researchers interested in addressing the impact of the Indian caste system on various aspects of society and exploring ways to promote equality and social justice.

International Efforts to Address Caste Discrimination

Caste discrimination in India has been an enduring issue, deeply rooted in the social fabric of the country. However, in recent years, there have been significant international efforts to address this pervasive problem and work towards creating a more equitable society. This subchapter will explore some of these initiatives and their impact on combating caste discrimination.

One notable international effort to address caste discrimination is the work of various human rights organizations and advocacy groups. These organizations, often in collaboration with local NGOs, aim to raise awareness about the issue and push for policy changes that promote equality and social justice. They engage with governments, international bodies, and other stakeholders to highlight the plight of marginalized communities affected by caste discrimination. Through their efforts, they seek to challenge discriminatory practices and promote inclusive policies.

Another important international initiative is the United Nations' engagement with the issue of caste discrimination. The UN has recognized caste discrimination as a form of racial discrimination and has actively worked towards its eradication. The UN's Special Rapporteur on contemporary forms of racism, racial discrimination, xenophobia, and related intolerance has documented and reported on caste-based discrimination in India, bringing international attention to the issue. This has led to increased pressure on the Indian government to take action and address this human rights concern.

Furthermore, international collaborations between academic institutions and scholars have played a crucial role in understanding and addressing caste discrimination. Sociologists from around the world have embarked on research projects, comparative studies, and knowledge exchange programs to gain insights into the Indian caste system and its implications for social inequality. This collective effort has contributed to a better understanding of the complexities of caste discrimination and its intersections with gender, class, and other forms of marginalization.

Additionally, the global community has witnessed the emergence of various movements and campaigns led by Dalit communities and civil society organizations. These movements have gained international attention and support, shedding light on the experiences of those affected by caste discrimination. Through protests, rallies, and social media campaigns, they have created awareness, challenged social norms, and demanded justice for the victims of caste-based discrimination.

While significant strides have been made, it is important to acknowledge that caste discrimination remains deeply entrenched in Indian society. International efforts, however, continue to play a vital role in highlighting the issue, fostering dialogue, and pressurizing the Indian government to take concrete steps towards eradicating caste discrimination. Through continued collaboration and advocacy, sociologists and other stakeholders can contribute to promoting equality, justice, and social cohesion in India and beyond.

Lessons from International Anti-Discrimination Movements

Introduction:

The fight against discrimination and social inequality has been a global struggle, with various movements and initiatives emerging across different countries. In this subchapter, we will explore the lessons that can be learned from international anti-discrimination movements and their relevance to understanding and combatting the Indian caste system. As sociologists, it is crucial to examine these movements and their impact on different aspects of society, such as access to education, the experiences of marginalized communities, and the perpetuation of social inequality.

Lessons for Access to Education:

International anti-discrimination movements have shown us that access to education is a key factor in challenging and dismantling discriminatory systems. By examining successful initiatives from other countries, we can gain insights into how educational opportunities can be expanded for marginalized communities in India. For example, strategies such as affirmative action and scholarships for disadvantaged groups have proven effective in promoting educational equality.

Lessons for Perpetuation of Social Inequality:

The experiences of other countries can provide valuable lessons on how the Indian caste system perpetuates social inequality. By studying the impact of discrimination in various contexts, we can identify common patterns and mechanisms that contribute to the marginalization of certain groups. This knowledge can help us develop targeted interventions to address the root causes of inequality within the Indian caste system.

Lessons for Intersectionality:

Examining the experiences of women and marginalized communities in other anti-discrimination movements can enhance our understanding of intersectionality within the Indian caste system. By recognizing the multiple layers of discrimination faced by individuals based on their caste, gender, and other social identities, we can better advocate for inclusive policies and empower those who face intersecting forms of oppression.

Lessons for Resistance Movements:

International examples of resistance movements against discrimination, such as the civil rights movement in the United States or anti-apartheid struggles in South Africa, can inspire and inform Dalit empowerment movements in India. By studying the strategies, successes, and challenges of these movements, we can gain insights into effective forms of resistance and mobilization against the Indian caste system.

Conclusion:

By drawing lessons from international anti-discrimination movements, sociologists can deepen their understanding of the Indian caste system and its impact on various aspects of society. These lessons can guide the development of more inclusive policies, empower marginalized communities, and ultimately contribute to the dismantling of the caste system and the promotion of equality in India. Through this exploration, we can gain valuable insights from the global fight against discrimination and apply them to the specific context of the Indian caste system.

Future Directions for Combating Caste-based Inequality

The Indian caste system has been a deeply rooted social structure for centuries, perpetuating inequality and marginalizing certain sections of society. However, as sociologists, we have a crucial role to play in addressing this issue and working towards a more equitable society. In this subchapter, we will explore the future directions for combating caste-based inequality in India.

One key area that demands attention is the impact of the Indian caste system on access to education. It is crucial to develop policies and interventions that promote equal educational opportunities for all individuals, regardless of their caste. This involves providing scholarships, affirmative action programs, and ensuring that schools and universities are inclusive and free from caste-based discrimination.

Furthermore, it is essential to recognize the intersectionality of caste and gender, as well as the experiences of marginalized communities. Women and other marginalized groups within the caste system face compounded discrimination and oppression. By understanding their unique experiences and challenges, we can develop targeted interventions and policies that address their specific needs.

Another important aspect to consider is the historical origins and evolution of the caste system. By delving into its roots, we can gain a deeper understanding of how it has perpetuated social inequality. This knowledge can inform efforts to challenge and dismantle the caste system's influence on various aspects of society.

The economic consequences of the caste system also require attention. It is crucial to address the disparities in wealth and opportunities that exist among different social classes. By promoting economic empowerment and providing skill development programs, we can help break the cycle of poverty and inequality perpetuated by the caste system.

Religious justifications and interpretations of the caste system also play a significant role in its perpetuation. It is necessary to engage with religious leaders and communities to challenge these justifications and promote a more inclusive and egalitarian interpretation of religious texts.

Furthermore, the influence of caste in politics and governance cannot be overlooked. Analyzing the role of caste in Indian elections and governance is crucial for understanding how it affects policy-making and representation. By advocating for inclusive and caste-neutral politics, we can work towards a more equitable society.

Dalit empowerment movements have played a crucial role in challenging the caste system and fighting for the rights and dignity of marginalized communities. It is important to support and amplify these movements, providing them with the resources and platforms they need to continue their resistance against caste-based discrimination.

Moreover, as the world becomes increasingly interconnected, the impact of globalization on the Indian caste system cannot be ignored. Exploring these dynamics and learning from international perspectives on caste discrimination and other forms of discrimination can provide new insights and strategies for combating inequality.

In conclusion, combating caste-based inequality requires a multifaceted approach that addresses education, gender, historical origins, economics, religion, politics, empowerment movements, globalization, and international perspectives. By actively engaging with these future directions, sociologists can contribute to the ongoing struggle for a more equitable and just society in India.

Target Audience: Sociologists

Subchapter Title: Target Audience: Sociologists

Introduction:

Welcome to the subchapter "Target Audience: Sociologists" of the book "Perpetuating Inequality: Exploring the Role of the Indian Caste System." This subchapter is specifically tailored for sociologists who are interested in gaining a comprehensive understanding of the Indian caste system and its various dimensions. As sociologists, you play a crucial role in analyzing, interpreting, and finding solutions to social problems. In this subchapter, we will delve into the intricate aspects of the Indian caste system, exploring its impact on education, perpetuation of social inequality, intersectionality, historical origins, economic consequences, religious justifications, political influence, resistance movements, globalization's impact, and international perspectives. By examining these topics, we aim to equip you with a profound understanding of the Indian caste system and its implications.

Content:

1. The impact of the Indian caste system on access to education:

This section will explore how the caste system limits educational opportunities for marginalized communities, hindering social mobility and perpetuating inequality.

2. The role of the Indian caste system in perpetuating social inequality:

Here, we will examine how the caste system serves as a structural barrier, shaping social hierarchies and reinforcing inequality across generations.

3. Intersectionality and the Indian caste system: examining the experiences of women and marginalized communities:

This section will analyze how gender and other intersecting identities intersect with caste, leading to unique experiences of discrimination and oppression.

4. The historical origins and evolution of the Indian caste system:

Understanding the historical context and evolution of the caste system is crucial to comprehend its deeply ingrained nature in Indian society.

5. The economic consequences of the Indian caste system on different social classes:

This section will explore how the caste system affects economic opportunities, income distribution, and socio-economic disparities among different caste groups.

6. Religious justifications and interpretations of the Indian caste system:

Examining the religious underpinnings of the caste system will shed light on its persistence and the challenges faced in eradicating it.

7. Caste-based politics: analyzing the influence of caste in Indian elections and governance:

We will discuss how caste-based politics shape electoral outcomes and governance in India, perpetuating divisions and hindering social progress.

8. Dalit empowerment movements and resistance against the Indian caste system:

This section will highlight the efforts made by marginalized communities, particularly Dalits, to challenge the caste system and fight for their rights and dignity.

9. The impact of globalization on the Indian caste system:

Globalization has both positive and negative consequences on the caste system. We will explore how it affects caste dynamics and the challenges it presents.

10. International perspectives on the Indian caste system: comparisons with other forms of discrimination:

Drawing comparisons with other forms of discrimination worldwide, this section will provide a broader understanding of the Indian caste system's uniqueness and universality.

Conclusion:

This subchapter is designed to provide sociologists with a comprehensive and nuanced understanding of the Indian caste system and its various dimensions. By examining its impact on education, perpetuation of social inequality, intersectionality, historical origins, economic consequences, religious justifications, political influence, resistance movements, globalization's impact, and international perspectives, we aim to equip sociologists with knowledge to address these complex issues and contribute to a more equitable society.